The Message of the Hands

Alternatives
Life Options for Today

Other titles in the *Alternatives* series are:

Astrology and Childhood Peter West
Dreams and Dreaming: Understanding Your Sleep Messages Tony Crisp
Educate Your Memory: Guidance for Students of All Ages Billy Roberts
Pen Pictures: Interpreting the Secrets of Handwriting Peter West
Personal Progress Through Positive Thinking Hilary Jones and Frank Gilbert
The Power of Peace: The Value of Meditation Shirley Wallis
Tarot for Today Ken Taylor
Visitation: The Certainty of Alien Activity Peter Hough
Working Memory: Improving Your Memory for the Workplace Billy Roberts

The Message of the Hands

PETER WEST

LONDON
HOUSE

First published in Great Britain in 2000 by
LONDON HOUSE
114 New Cavendish Street
London W1M 7FD

A catalogue record for this book is available
from the British Library

ISBN 1 902809 28 9

Edited and designed by DAG Publications Ltd, London.
Printed and bound by Biddles Limited,
Guildford, Surrey.

Contents

Introduction　7

Part One: Chirognomy　13
1. The Shape of the Hand　14
2. The Square or Useful Hand　18
3. The Conic or Artistic Hand　22
4. The Spatulate or Active Hand　26
5. The Philosophic or Knotty Hand　30
6. The Psychic or Idealist Hand　34
7. The Elementary or Basic Hand　38
8. The Mixed Hand　42
9. Fire, Earth, Air and Water Hands　46
10. The Back of the Hands　50
11. The Nails　54
12. The Fingers　58
13. The Thumb　66
14. The Mounts of the Hand　70

75   **Part Two: Chiromancy**

76   15. The Lines on the Hand

81   16. The Head Line

87   17. The Heart Line

92   18. The Life Line

97   19. The Fate Line

103   20. The Minor Lines

112   21. Special Marks and Signs

118   22. How to Time Events

123   **Part Three: Dermatoglyphics –
      The Skin Patterns**

124   23. The Digital Patterns

133   24. The Palmar Patterns

139   25. Handprints

142   Further reading

143   Index

Introduction

Palmistry probably began in the east. India is the most likely source, for most of the oldest documentation, much with graphic illustrations, originates from there.

Of all the references we have at present, these works pre-date just about everything else. We know palmistry was practised in Japan, Korea and China at around the same period, so it is fairly safe to assume that hand reading of one kind or another was quite widely known about 5,000–5,500 years ago in the east.

However, in the western world we were unaware of palmistry until much later, certainly in writing. The main problem was in recording such things. Because few people could write, and even fewer were able to read, records of esoteric origins were at a premium.

In Britain and on the European continent there are a handful or so of very rare references, but they are not that easy to date. In these olden times, palmistry was considered as superstition or magic. There were no firm rules for any student to learn, so no organised system could be passed down through the years. But as I have just remarked, very few were sufficiently educated to read or write anyway. Such matters would have taken up far too much time for the small handful of scribes who were available to make records of any kind.

In England, reading and writing as a matter of course for the ordinary citizen came into being about 150–200 years ago. Previously, it was only people in religious orders or the rich who were taught such skills.

Subjects like palmistry and astrology were a long way down the list of priorities of those who could read and write, but there is some documented proof that palmistry was understood by the Greeks and Romans as early as 240 BC. The great Aristotle is alleged to have written a short treatise. This suggests that palmistry was probably quite ancient even then.

Throughout history, there are many references to hands in medical diagnoses written by astrologers. In those early days because these two disciplines seem to be so interwoven, some of the observations made then are still used today, much modified by our greater understanding of such matters, of course.

Early English documentation is sketchy, not so much for a lack of knowledge, but for an inability to set down in writing anything clear-cut. The main difficulty was a plain and simple communication problem. Before the Norman Conquest in 1066, the official language in this country was Old English. It differed dialectically from area to area because the country was divided into many little kingdoms. Just prior to 1066, written Latin began to be used, but by very few people. What was written was created in the abbeys, churches and monasteries by monks. The ordinary person could hardly speak their own local dialect.

Soon after the Battle of Hastings, many of the Normans and their continental allies were appointed to important positions in these same abbeys, monasteries and regional seats of authority where it now made sense to continue to write everything in Latin. It was practical, too.

None of the old languages of Britain or any of the new Norman ones were exactly compatible: direct conversation between the conquered and the conquerors was not easy. At about this time, it became the practice of the new lords to write a decree in their own language and pass it to the scribes, who first translated it into Latin, then into the Anglo-Saxon tongue(s) of the region.

There were no rules of grammar and, of course, no teachers who could instruct how this should be done. The monks and scribes, who were still largely the writers of the day, had no set methods or prin-ciples for setting things down. This would not occur for nearly two to three centuries.

Thus, one can see how palmistry could not even be considered as a fit subject let alone be expected to take precedence over any – or all – of the local and countrywide decrees the new masters issued so prolifically.

One other big stumbling block remained – the Church. It was in the middle of many changes trying to convert ordinary people from the old religions in order to maintain its hold and authority. The then established Church wielded much power. It opposed palmistry and astrology as the work of the Devil partly because they were then inextricably linked and because many traditional terms in hand reading are basically astrological.

From those times we are able to trace many errors. In those days, the terminologies of astrology and palmistry were thought to be the same, but they were not, perhaps another contributory cause for why so little material is available from the period.

With the advent of the printing press, around the middle of the 15th century, the beginning of some printed matter became available in England and Europe.

It is important also to remember that palmistry was mostly a one-to-one interview in those times and probably conducted in secret. Whatever was said between any two people during such a session was almost never recorded at the same time.

If a record was made, it would have been some time after the event and almost certainly by someone who was not present. This is yet another reason why there was no properly recorded history made, and why what we do have is so sketchy.

In England, there followed a short period where very little to do with palmistry seems to have happened. If anything did occur, it was shrouded in secrecy, but on the Continent palmistry began to gain currency.

There were probably two reasons. Palmistry was still viewed as the work of the Devil by many and associated with the gypsies, a people who were never really quite trusted. What they represented was not what proper society wanted. Among many other things, astrology and palmistry seemed to be a mainstay of these itinerant nobodies, mostly quacks or hangers-on at fairs and fêtes. They swarmed around army camps. What tradition that did exist was handed down by word of mouth.

Gypsies first appeared in England in the fourteenth century, but by 1530 they had earned themselves such a terrible reputation that a royal decree was made by Henry VIII. He wrote about them, "An outlandish people who call themselves Egyptians have come into my realm in great companies and who have committed many heinous felonies and robberies".

That hurt the gypsies. It did them no good at all, for to be one and to get caught on the the wrong side of the law meant death. This statute by Henry VIII was not repealed until the reign of George III (1760–1820).

This is all very helpful historically, for it meant that if these gypsies were Egyptians, then they were well versed in palmistry prior to

9

fleeing their country in the early sixteenth century because of political and religious troubles. However, some writers claim the "Egyptians" were from India, where there was always political in-fighting.

It was also thought that palmistry was virtually non-existent in Egypt, whereas in India it was highly respected as a popular and well-known practice by all and sundry, whatever their social rank.

That gypsies introduced palmistry to Britain is wrong, for all the early documentation proves it. Nevertheless, it is probably the persecution by Henry VIII that provided the fuel for the fire of this belief and quite possibly a reason for the still common distrust of gypsies in many rural areas of Britain today.

In the middle of the 17th century, George Wharton, a publisher of almanacs, produced a translation of the work of a continental palmist called Rothmann. In 1653, one of Wharton's friends and associates, Richard Saunders, published a palmistry book called *Physiognomie, and Chiromancie, Metoscopie*. These books were milestones in English publishing that went a long way to help popularise hand reading.

Wharton was a friend of Elias Ashmole, who was later raised to the peerage for his efforts on behalf of Charles II in the Civil War. Saunders was also a good friend of William Lilly, the astrologer. They belonged to another group and tended to work independently, but helped to change the course of palmistry and astrology in England.

Saunders' first work was mainly original, the result of his own research and study. However, it also included wholesale copying of the works of the French palmist Jean Belot.

Later, in 1664 Saunders published what is now regarded as one of the most invaluable works for any student, partly because of the way it reflects the thinking of the time. His *Palmistry, the Secrets Disclosed* is held in great respect. Much of what he wrote then is still observed today, but, once again, modified by modern thinking.

At about the same time, John Bulwer wrote the first known English language book on how to use the hand and hand gestures for communicating with the deaf. As time has passed, there have been many works in countless languages to promote the cause of palmists everywhere. However, it was not until after the middle of the 19th century that a sudden rise to prominence occurred. It quickly became fashionable to have your hands read or bumps felt. People visited early graphologists and consulted with astrologers quite openly.

This was the age of discovery. The Victorians loved anything new and adventurous. Gadgets galore were everywhere, and claims for this and that abounded. If anyone knew how to con, misrepresent, pass-off, plagiarise or steal anything, it was during late Victorian times.

If it caught the public fancy, there was always someone, somewhere, who could improve or claim glory for their findings or systems. People everywhere fell over themselves to jump on the bandwagon of just about everything. Palmistry was no exception. Without doubt, the real winners were those involved in all the different characterology studies. Individuals are the same everywhere: they love to hear about themselves.

As the 20th century dawned, Count Louis Hamon, who used the name of Cheiro, dominated the palmistry scene. The most successful of his time, he read hands brilliantly and wrote books that are still considered to be landmarks of palmistry.

Cheiro had the gift of seership and was a clever numerologist with a good working knowledge of astrology. He was an Irishman, born in Dublin on November 1, 1886. But there was another side to him that the public did not know about: he was an egomaniac, complete with a highly inventive imagination.

In fairness, it is better to remember his achievements in hand reading rather than dwell on his other activities. There are many accounts of his life and adventures that, to say the least, are dramatically entertaining but not entirely truthful. In essence, Cheiro was one of the world's first super-salesmen. He could sell just about anything – and that included himself.

Nevertheless, his first book, *The Language of the Hand*, published when he was in his late twenties, was brilliant and made him a star. In some cases, perhaps, stars can be forgiven for a few of their wayward actions when they go beyond the pale.

From here on, there are so many who have contributed to palmistry we cannot mention them all. Before we leave this brief survey, we should not forget the first – and probably still the best – of all American palmists.

William Benham published his classic, *The Laws of Scientific Hand Reading*, in 1900, and it was an instant success. Known as "the palmists' bible", it is over 600 pages long, crammed solid with facts and an absolute must for any student of hand reading.

11

Palmistry became more of a national matter at about this time as individual palmists worked either alone in their own country or with others abroad. Thus, in the last 100 years or so tremendous advances in all aspects of hand analysis have been made in many different countries.

Some have led to radical changes of medical opinion, perhaps none more so than when in the 1960s an English hospital experimented with the taking of hand-prints of newborn babies with suspected Down's syndrome. This produced most encouraging results, and led to other similar studies.

This experiment spurred others to re-appraise hand reading not just for this, but for other ills and problems then alleged to be detected from the hand. Some police forces began to palm-print as well as finger-print a few suspects and use character studies supplied by palmists, which led to good recorded results.

Today, large businesses and other companies with enlightened human resources managers who appreciate the input of their staff now regularly utilise the services of a hand analyst or a handwriting expert in selection/promotion exercises. Their success rate speaks for itself. Unfortunately, this is not always admitted by these organisations, perhaps for fear of ridicule. Nevertheless, slowly and surely, it is becoming more widespread.

Palmistry, at long last, has become respectable.

Part One
CHIROGNOMY

1

The Shape of the Hand

The hand should be regarded as a three-dimensional map. Long before you begin to examine the lines and skin patterns, you have first to establish the kind of terrain upon which they are found.

If you think of the lines as railway tracks, you need to appreciate that certain areas over which they have been laid must wield some influence over their individual interpretation.

Imagine the view from the carriage window when the train you are on passes through a long, open valley: you see everything. But if you pass through a heavily wooded area, you get to view precious little.

In palmistry, lines take on slightly different meanings according to the type of hand and the nature of the area on which they are to be found. This is a most important feature of hand analysis.

When you begin to assess the type of the hand you are presented with, you will find there is an astonishing amount of information to be found from just the shape alone.

Although it is agreed that there are only two basic shapes, the square and the conic (or round), it is accepted that from them we recognise the seven hand shapes of traditional palmistry. These other shapes are variations on the original square or round. As we progress, it will be seen that these traditional classifications can often seem to be misleading because, strictly speaking, they refer to the whole hand.

Most modern palmists tend to classify the palmar area only. In many ways this makes sense. Fingers, too, are classified into types: they may be square-tipped, pointed, spatulate, round or conic. Conic is an old word for round. The term is still in use today by many palmists.

Basic shapes
To determine the shape of a hand, look at the palmar surface from the base of the fingers down to the wrist and note whether the outer edge, the percussion, is curved or straight.

If it appears square, then classify it as such. If it seems to look slightly rounded, it is a conic palm.

Sometimes the hand seems slightly wider at the wrist than at the base of the fingers, or the other way round, wider at the top of the palm and narrower at the wrist. This is called the spatulate hand.

The fingers may seem long and bony with clearly defined bulges at each of the phalangeal joints. This is the philosophical hand. If the fingers are long and pointed with a long, narrow palm, it is the psychic hand.

Occasionally, you will see a hand that looks quite basic – a short, squat palm, stubby little fingers with a thumb that may have been stuck on as an afterthought. This is the elementary hand.

It is quite possible to have round fingers on a square or round palm, or square fingers on a square or round palm. There may be a selection of fingertips, in which case it is the mixed hand.

This exercise calls for keen observation right from the start and never stops. It is not always easy at the beginning, but you will be surprised at how quickly everything falls into place once you have had some experience at classifying hand shapes.

Initially, it takes a lot of practice and patience, but do not be afraid to experiment on those around you. Look at your own hands, but try to be as impartial as possible when doing so. If unsure, get someone else to do it for you.

Approach the exercise with common sense, remembering that there are no hidden or occult meanings to try to decipher.

Palmar/finger length

Next, judge the length of the fingers in relation to the length of the palm. If it is not immediately apparent, they may be of equal length, give or take a couple of centimetres or so. Often, the palm is longer than the fingers.

To be certain, measure the length of the palm from where it joins the wrist up to the crease at the base of the middle finger. If it is clear enough to be seen, use the end of the skin pattern or the top rascette or bracelet, one of the lines across the wrist.

Now measure the length of the middle finger from top to bottom. When the finger is longer than the palm, the fingers are judged as long in comparison because, as a rule, the middle finger is the longest. This is usually obvious.

Where the palm is clearly longer than the fingers, then they must be adjudged as short fingers.

The thumb

Now assess the size of thumb in relation to the whole hand. It should always look as though it belongs to the hand. A large, heavy thumb can offset a routine assessment of the type of hand, as would a poor weak-looking affair that seems as if it has been stuck on the side of the hand at the last moment.

The mounts

These are the small areas or pads whose development or otherwise permits extra insight into the character and personality of the subject. Having said that, it is fair to say that certain palmists tend to ignore them completely. Some give them a passing thought or two while others study them long and hard, and always include them in their final assessment.

The small padded areas found at the base of each of the fingers and the thumb are referred to as digital mounts. Mounts are also to be found along the percussion or outer edge of the palm. Between the thumb and the forefinger on both the front and the back of the hand are two more mounts.

Each of the mounts are named after the traditional gods of old, and are, in turn, associated with astrology. Perhaps it is here more than anywhere else in hand reading that the links with astrology are at their strongest.

There are a few small details to fill in with regard to the shape and parts of the hand, but they are more properly included in the section in which they are found.

The nails

When you look at the backs of anyone's hands you should observe the colour, shape and size of the nails, though not necessarily in this order. Nails are very important, for they indicate the subject's present state of health.

From a study of the nails you will be able to assess the amount of stress, strain and nervous tension, and how the vascular system is currently standing up to it all. You should always keep a weather eye on your nails because when under stress, you may note changes in them and can take the necessary remedial actions.

Once you have these elementary measurements and assessments clear in your mind, you are ready to start a basic interpretation. In the following pages are in-depth studies of all the individual parts of the hand. The lines and skin patterns will be dealt with later.

2

The Square or Useful Hand

For better accuracy, one should assess the shape of hand from the front or palmar side because often the hand can seem to be one shape if looked at from the back of the hand, but something quite different when turned round.

If in appearance the hand seems square, rectangular or oblong, then that is the basic shape. Curiously enough, many hands often seem to look square when viewed from the back anyway.

The outer edge of the hand looks straight; the base of the hand at the wrist has a similar appearance. The fingers at the top of the palm may appear to be arched, sloping or evenly set. Often, the first and fourth fingers can be set much lower.

Fingers may appear long, short, thick, thin, straight or crooked, but in spite of all these variations, should the whole hand – and that includes the fingers – look square, once again you must classify it as such.

The square hand is more often than not called "the useful hand". It is to be found everywhere. People with this hand shape tend to be practical, conventional and rather set in their ways. These folk are able to undertake all those little practical tasks that other, less practically gifted individuals are unable to do.

Such characters are logical and methodical: they demonstrate endless patience, usually coupled with level-headedness. They can also be quite determined – and extremely stubborn when they choose!

As a rule, almost anything new and untried is likely to be viewed with suspicion. They tend to resist change because they look upon it as unnecessary. Many are often unhappy with the unknown and in extreme cases probably fear it. As a rule, they maintain that if something works well there is no point in making changes, a logic that appeals to quite a few irrespective of hand shape.

People with square hands rarely show affection in public, although they feel things just as deeply as other folk. If they are to

Note the straight percussion. The whole hand gives an
impression of being square

be faulted, it is with their emotions and their imaginations. Generally, there are few lines on square palms.

While they remain in control, especially of themselves, there is no problem. When changes are imminent, they do not like to be seen to make mistakes. They worry about loss of control, for they can become so anxious when unsure of their ground.

If changes are introduced, it takes them a long time to adapt to the new or improved system. Changes of any kind are, therefore, to be opposed in their eyes, but if you give them long enough, they can – and do – eventually adapt.

Square-handed people are conventional and extremely self-reliant, with a healthy respect for authority, law and order – the right way of doing things. They are punctual and orderly, always willing to take positions of authority when offered, for they have a sense of responsibility second to none.

These are the doers of this world, often called the "salt of the earth", for society can build on their shoulders. They know how to delegate, how to organise, and how to bring law and order, method and calm, where chaos might otherwise rule.

They are not so much argumentative as stubborn when in the throes of what they know or believe to be right. They have a strong love of discipline and order, and automatically take their place in the hierarchy of things.

Those with square hands are not resigned to this as such, but because they are out-and-out materialists, they automatically conform with a habit they instinctively recognise as one who knows their place in life. It is rare for them to demonstrate affection in public, and when doing so they tend to keep half an eye open for who is watching at the time. They feel very deeply, but prefer to keep their real, inner feelings to themselves.

Such characters make extremely loyal friends and always insist on keeping alive the family traditions. As it is important for them not to lose track of their relatives, they always strive to keep the family united.

They make excellent hosts, for their main concern is to entertain and see that guests fully enjoy themselves. These folk also make very good, loyal employees or employers.

Abstract thinking is not really their forte at all. They are well out of their depth when it comes to idealistic subjects such as religion, psychology or artistic appreciation.

They are unable to take anything to any extreme in their way of thinking because their philosophy simply cannot grasp what is not physically there. This does not mean that they are unable to think things through. Far from it, but they cannot translate idealism or theory into any practical everyday usage.

Finger shapes
Fingers can be long or short, or thick or thin. They may be square or round, spatulate, pointed, knotted or smooth. A "mixed" set of fingers might also be seen on a square hand. Whatever is found on a square palm tempers the basic interpretation.

If someone's fingers are long and square, then the imaginative side of his or her nature will be more active, the mind much more open to new ideas.

Short, square fingers show an impulsive streak, but on a square hand someone who rarely makes the same mistake twice. He or she will have a good sense of business. People with hands like this are also stubborn.

It is rare to see long and pointed fingers on a square palm, but when present the nature is far more idealistic. The spirit is almost always willing, but the body can lag behind!

It is similar with short, pointed fingers. In this case, much may be started, but little is finished. Long conic fingers make the owner more inclined to be artistic and practical. These folk make useful things that are also worthwhile.

The round but short-fingered person needs to be kept busy. They lack concentration and usually have only a passing interest in what is going on around them, but often have a strongly intuitive side to their nature.

Long spatulate fingers make the person inventive, practical and innovative. People with short spatulate fingers enjoy making all sorts of things and are often to be found involved in gardening, agricultural or other outdoor pursuits.

Long fingers with knots at the phalange joints imply a pedantic nature, always concerned with detail. These people are able to conceive, create and use things with the greatest of ease.

Short knotted fingers are not often seen, but when present the subject will be over-critical and stubborn. You really do have to be very sure of your facts when you oppose them.

People with smooth fingers – those without knotting at the joints – absorb information very easily, while folk with long fingers tend to think a little more before taking action. Individuals with short, smooth fingers are extremely impulsive. They will start things before they have the complete story – and that often costs them dearly.

A mixed set of long fingers suggests versatility, those able to turn their hands to anything once their mind is made up. However, mixed short fingers are always so full of ideas they rarely seem to have much in the way of follow through. Literally, they have too many fingers in too many pies all at the same time. As a result, they are unable to concentrate for long on single issues.

Most people who have square hands, whatever the variations, are largely practical, well ordered and creatures of habit. They dream and have great ambitions like everyone else but, for most of the time, keep their feet firmly on the ground. They let others take the lead and think for them.

3
The Conic or Artistic Hand

When the palm and fingers are both conic, the whole hand has a slight tapering effect. Both edges of the hand should look soft in comparison to a square hand. The outer edge of the palm has a quite definite curve to it. People with this hand shape are very creative and artistic.

It also implies an impulsive and idealistic nature. These folk are liable to make or break any association easily, although not because they are unfeeling. Far from it. But they must have the constant stimulus of change. Anything new and untried is always welcome. They have to stay on the move, for they can be so destructive when at a loose end with nothing to do: there is a low boredom threshold. There is little love for tradition: it is the fascination of the new that attracts. They are well-known for trying anything once – twice if they like it!

Mostly, their knowledge tends to be superficial. They can talk fluently and convincingly on so many different topics, but it does not take long for an observer to note that there is no real depth to their knowledge. The life and soul of any party, they are the first to break the ice, play a game or get up and dance. If it should flag, it will not be for long. So if you want any gathering to go with a swing, put a conic hand on your planning committee.

Often, there is an inherent lazy streak and they can be selfish. Moody, imaginative, these people bounce back from set-backs with great facility, full of their special charm and personal magnetism.

However, in close emotional associations, they are likely to be changeable and, in extreme cases, totally inconsistent. They are not shallow. It is just that they get so involved with the mood of the moment that all else is put to one side until the affair cools. Then the cycle starts all over again. The real fault here is that these people probably fall in love with love more than anything else, for they are so very impressionable.

Creative – although not necessarily in the sense of a musician, painter, poet, sculptor or writer – they have a natural gift for the artistic side of life one way or another.

Retaining some semblance of personal discipline is difficult and for some it can be a serious problem. It is hard to call a halt to anything that brings a reward. Easily distracted, they find it difficult to sustain their concentration for long periods even when it is necessary.

If the palm is firm to the touch, impulsiveness eases a little, willpower becomes slightly more resolute and the subject has a firmer, more mature outlook on life.

A strong, square-tipped thumb would help here, for then these artistic and creative talents would become better employed more sensibly, and in a business-like manner. There would be much less idealism and far more practicality.

When the hand is firm to the touch or the fingers are longer than the palm, there will be a significant increase in their ability to deal with matters involving detail. They are better able to use their talents to influence others, but constructively so. This is like the actor or politician known for his eloquence which, when combined with a genuine or contrived emotion, can be really most persuasive.

Finger shapes
Fingers are either long or short, or thick, thin, square, round, spatulate, pointed, knotted or smooth. Like a square hand, round-handed people can also have mixed fingers. In just the same way as the square hand, they tend to help modify basic meanings.

Square fingers are not often seen on a round palm, but when they are, there will be strong reasoning powers with a much better control over their emotional outlook. There is more persistence. Artistic matters are more practically interpreted, like interior decorating, for example.

With pointed fingers, inspiration and idealism are a strong point. These people know how to achieve, how to apply themselves and win. On a round hand, the palm will probably be soft to the touch. This suggests opportunism and a lazy streak. A palm firm to the touch is unusual, but on the plus side it helps to strengthen the intuitive nature.

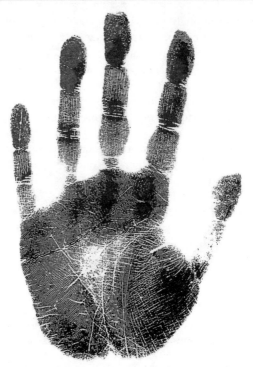

Note the rounded overall appearance, especially the curve on the percussion.

Fingers knotted at the joints of the phalanges indicate a rather better than average attention to detail. In some cases, it can border on the over-fussy; everything has to be just so. There may be a restricted imagination: whatever captures their fancy at the time needs a practical element to go with it.

When the fingers are spatulate, the owner never tires of mental or physical activities and rarely baulks at anything new. Indeed, they actively encourage it. They love to experiment with the tried and trusted. If left alone long enough, they might well discover a new way of doing something that has served well for years. The firmer the palm, the more inventive the owner.

A soft palm inclines the owner to procrastination. He or she will leave everything to the last moment, not so much through any lazy streak, but because they thrive on pressure. There is a very low boredom threshold, and when in this mood, these people can be quite destructive.

When there are mixed fingers on a conic hand, expect the owner to display a lot of emotional dependence on someone. They do not like to be left on their own for any length of time, and do not always learn from their mistakes. Such folk are very sensitive to criticism, no matter how well meant it may be.

They worry inwardly, far too much for their own good really. And if the palm is soft, they walk and talk themselves into all kinds of scrapes because of their insatiable curiosity streak. But they are also survivors, rarely completely losing everything.

In essence, people with round or conic hands are optimists, often quite enthusiastic and always lively, give or take the prevailing mood and circumstances. This makes them very attracted by – and attractive to – the opposite sex. Many romantic encounters are the norm, but they are not so much over-sexed as just natural targets for others who see them as potentially exciting partners.

There is no serious malice in the overall make-up despite an inbuilt selfish streak. But having made that point, these people can put their pleasures to one side to help the less fortunate. If they do decide to help you out with a favour, you must be in their good books. You will almost certainly have to pay them back just when you least expect it.

It is at times like these you would do well not only to remember how unreliable they can be, but also how engaging and well-meaning, too. In the case of conic hands, this is not always a comfort!

4

The Spatulate or Active Hand

Normally, the spatulate hand is a variation of the square shape and is not often seen to stem from the basically conic hand, but just occasionally this does occur.

The spatulate hand appears more rectangular than square, but what clearly identifies it is a defined widening either at the base of the palm, where it joins the wrist, or where the fingers spring from the top of the palm.

Usually, but not necessarily, each of the fingers is liable to look spatulated at its tip. They may bulge slightly, irrespective of the shape of the nail when viewed from the back of the hand.

This hand always indicates extreme restlessness: the owners must always be doing something. They are often highly-strung, full of nervous energy and quite likely to seem eccentric when first you meet them. Expect to find some level of the unconventional or at the very least a natural rebellious streak.

These types enjoy their independence. In fact, they may insist on it. He or she is likely to be greatly innovative, with a natural talent for inventiveness. They love tinkering with almost anything that can be taken apart. Such folk would change the world if given half a chance.

Rarely satisfied, they cannot stay still in one place for long. These characters have to be doing something to keep themselves occupied and cannot abide inactivity.

One of the best descriptions of relaxing for them is to read a book while listening to the radio, perhaps knitting and with at least one eye watching television. Should the phone ring, there is no problem, for that would add to life's little excitements for them.

They all have an inbuilt streak of ingenuity. If given long enough, they will create an entirely new method of doing something, often more economically, too.

The spatulate hand type is not always physically strong, partly because they have a mental approach to life. Many enjoy manual dexterity. This can be enhanced if they are also naturally left-handed. There are few truly ambidextrous people, but when you do find one, he or she often has spatulated palms, finger and thumb tips.

If the spatulation is at the base of the hand, the owner is likely to be mentally astute, perceptive and very quick-witted. When the the upper part of the hand is wider, a more practical approach to life will be demonstrated all the time.

It is rare to find a spatulate hand as an extension of the round or conic shape, but it does happen. There is a need, therefore, to study this particular hand carefully to classify it correctly.

When the spatulate hand is a development of the round hand shape, expect to find practical artistic gifts. Music, drama or both may appeal. There might also be writing ability, not so much as a writer of fiction, more a technical author, perhaps. But if these types were to write fiction, the subject matter might be on something out of the ordinary and unusual.

When the fingers are long, especially the little finger, there will be good communicating skills, a gift for oratory, public speaking, lecturing or perhaps politics.

Strangely, there is often poor dress sense. It may be eccentric or unusual, or just a plain, old-fashioned inability to make a sensible colour match. In some cases, such people can be known more for this character quirk than anything else.

There is one very off-putting trait – a strong love for working behind the scenes, to act in secrecy. These people have such a great love of the mysterious. Stage magicians with spatulate hands always have that little bit extra in their act.

Nevertheless, as far as ordinary people are concerned, provided you allow these rather personal but unusual idiosyncrasies, treat them without much scepticism and deal with them honestly at all times, you will have a good, reliable friend or partner.

Spatulate hands indicate a strong element of resourcefulness. This is an active, industrious character who thoroughly enjoys fighting through petty bureaucracy, red tape and similar kinds of obstacles to achieve his ambition. He always responds well to challenges. To him, life is just one huge adventure to be indulged as he sees fit.

Women with these hands are often found working in the medical or scientific worlds. They are blessed with the energy and endurance necessary for such work. As they also have plenty of common sense,

27

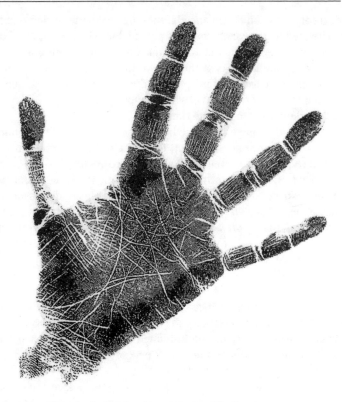

*The palm is slightly wider at the top. The fingers are
wide spread, suggesting activity*

many of them make excellent nurses, but are equally at home on a
building site as an architect or an engineer.

Good travellers at all times, they relish a fondness for sport,
preferably individual or direct competition activities rather than in
a team. Further, they are also very good pilots and efficient officers
on board ships. They make excellent entertainers, too, preferably as
an individual artiste, musician or singer while others excel as
actresses.

Almost without exception they prize independence and
freedom more than anything. Some will flout the law, and even
break it to achieve their aims. Others simply re-write the rules to
suit themselves.

Many are just natural-born revolutionaries who openly and actively oppose law and order. However, they do not actually incite rebellion in the political sense. Mostly, all they want is a society where they can freely express their ideas without the confines of convention.

People with spatulate hands and spatulate tips to their fingers all have an added zest and enthusiasm for life. When the fingers are smooth, opulence and all things rich and elegant attract.

If the fingers are knotted (developed) at the joints, then the subject will exhibit an almost tyrannical approach to life. They can be most ruthless when in a position of power and often ignore even the basic humanities as an employer. If their fingertips are pointed, religious idealism, philosophy and educational matters attract. The occult and the unknown fascinate them.

With conic, or round fingers, there will be a definite practical artistic streak: painting, pottery, even sculpting. With wide or broad hands, this is likely to extend to outdoor pursuits such as landscape gardening or farming.

With square-tipped fingers, there is always a strong practical streak in the make-up. Almost a second nature, this is the mark of the craftsman, practically creative like a carpenter or an engineer, or anything where they can make things with the hands.

5

The Philosophic or Knotty Hand

This hand looks square or slightly rectangular and is rather bony with fingers that always have clearly defined knuckles and bulges at each of the phalangeal joints.

In its pure form, a philosophic hand is rectangular from the tips of the fingers to the wrist. The palm can sometimes look a trifle squeezed while the fingers seem thin. The rather prominent knotty knuckles tend to emphasise this.

Fingertips may be conic or round, pointed, spatulate or square, but never thick or blunt-looking. As a rule, the nails are long, wide and sensibly trimmed: they are rarely small and wide.

The thumbs will be low-set with well-balanced first and second phalanges of equal length, the latter seemingly "waisted" in its appearance. Additionally, the thumbs almost always look large for the size of the hands on which they feature.

The knotty hand seems to be made up of a square palm with knotty fingers, but this is not so. Technically, the philosophic hand is a mixture of the square and conic shapes. As such shapes are funda-mentally opposite in their nature, these people really take some understanding. In rare cases, the left hand may be square and the right one round, or vice versa.

People with hands like this experience things very deeply. Almost without exception they prefer their own company and cannot really be considered social animals.

This hand suggests a certain amount of refinement and an innate sensitivity that seems to imply a mental approach. Often, these people lack robust health, so any physical activity is more likely to be determined by the mind.

In essence, theirs is a lone-wolf mentality: they are inclined to live their lives to their own satisfaction. Few people understand them and even fewer actually try, so they tend to be left to their own devices. Equally, few people can cope with them and even fewer are able to live with them. It takes the patience of a saint and the wisdom of Solomon to partner them!

However, despite all this, they are far from anti-social. While perhaps shunning an active social life, they are cultured, refined, shrewd and most entertaining when dealing with family, friends or work colleagues.

If – and it is a big if – they decide to turn on the charm, you will also find excellent manners with a perceptive, mischievous, even impish sense of fun. These folk have "presence". They are dignified and usually dress well.

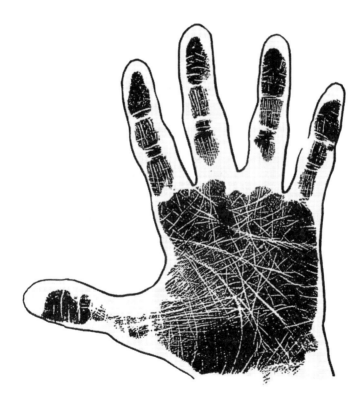

Note the prominent bulging or knotting on the bottom finger joints. It is less obvious on the top phalanges. The thumb is very strong.

What they advise, say or do should be observed and noted. These people are often found in education, religion, science or the social sciences. Mostly, it is the politics that attract as they love the cut-and-thrust of debate.

It is rare to see them demonstrate public acts of affection, for such displays of emotion are not for them. They are not unfeeling. Far from it, for these types can be quite ardent and very sensual. However, everything has its place. They are genuinely sincere and very sentimental. Because they are so intensely loyal and such idealists that they are not easily swayed by others, you would have to be silver-tongued and very persuasive indeed to effect any change in their beliefs or considered courses of action.

Despite all this idealism, in their later life they are nearly always materially successful. They have a knack of acquiring and accumulating possessions and assets. It is not all dreaming and scheming, though: they thrive on facts, enjoy research work and are always prepared to work things out for themselves.

Some can seem awfully slow at times, but they are always so sure, and their need to study, to gain knowledge and to validate things is something of a second nature.

Theirs is a world of order and precision, occasionally at the expense of emotional considerations. Good at lateral thinking, they arrive at the nub of a problem very quickly. Then their whole personality undergoes a change and they become so absorbed with the project that it may even be to the exclusion of all else. Some can find them unapproachable and difficult to understand. Frankly, they are best left alone to their own devices to enjoy their life their way.

As a rule, the knotty hand is firm to the touch, the skin texture fine. This shows activity and tenacity of purpose. But should the hand be soft to the touch, the mind does not delve too deeply into academic matters.

The prominences or knotting found at the phalangeal joints of the fingers may be regarded as a check on the flow of incoming ideas. When knots are found between the first and second phalange (the top joint), it shows a slow and difficult-to-please character with a strongly critical nature.

If the joint between the second and base phalange is accentuated, self-discipline is more rigorously applied, actions and thoughts more methodical. The nature is very tidy, orderly and pragmatic.

With both joints emphasised, it is a sign of the real sceptic – cold, calculating and very precise, the true philosophic hand. If with pointed fingertips, the owner is exceptionally idealistic. Spiritual matters and religious affairs attract and may dominate life.

If the fingertips are spatulate, the subject is more materially-minded. Large basal phalanges suggest the gourmand, but if thin, he or she may be more of a gourmet. Either way, they have sensual natures.

With square fingertips, the owner is more realistic and useful to know, for they have a down-to-earth, practical approach to life. Often, there is an affinity for all types of mathematics and the sciences; indeed, anything that requires precision. With older folk, a love of ceremony and ritual will have developed.

Round or conic tips suggest an interest in esotericism. So-called occult subjects, astrology or similar characterology arts/sciences attract: many make excellent and perceptive numerologists.

The thumb on the philosophic hand is often large, which indicates just how dominant and forceful these people can be when pursuing an ambition. However, if the thumb is on the small side, then they will be more intuitive and one can sense that feelings can – and do – influence decisions.

Because these individuals are so often found among the leaders in society, they are often the authors as well as the auditors of our style of life. In reality, we achieve very little without their influence being felt somewhere.

6

The Psychic or Idealist Hand

This hand shape, while fairly rare in this day and age, is always instantly recognisable. It is usually an extreme version of the round or conic hand. The palm is long and slim, and has slender, narrow fingers that taper delicately to a point.

These hands are always beautifully kept. The owners tend to have immaculate, almond-shaped nails that create a soft and rather genteel appearance.

This hand indicates someone who lives a life in a state of almost total mental and emotional idealism. They are not really suited to the cut-and-thrust of the busy, harsh, modern world in which we live today. As a result, such folk are rather rarely seen.

They are not practical and have almost no business sense, either. Always willing to trust everything and everyone a little bit too readily, they confide in all the wrong people for all the wrong reasons. This leads to all manner of problems, with them being deeply hurt, often without realising why.

Unfortunately, they fail to learn by their mistakes and suffer similar occurrences repeatedly. These idealistic visionaries are better off as far away as possible from the realities of what we call the normal world.

However, there are a few saving graces. If the hand has a good, strong thumb or a palm firm to the touch, a much tougher nature will be present, making them more practical, and, therefore, better suited to everyday life.

When placed in a position of authority, they are able to bring into play an innate gift of diplomacy and tact, and make wonderful arbitrators. If they are involved in negotiations and rule against you, they make it seem as though it is the right thing to do. Other gifts include culture, taste and discernment in the food, wine, health, hygiene and jewellery worlds.

People with psychic hands often have small bulges or "droplets", which show quite clearly on the palmar side of the fingertips. These small configurations signify a highly developed sense of touch and "taste". This tends to exaggerate the sense of refinement, certainly when the subject has a special talent in any one particular direction.

Ideally, perhaps if all the fingers had these sensitivity pads the owners would be universally known for their very special talents. But as a rule, they tend to appear on only one or two fingers and just occasionally on the thumb.

The position of the sensitivity pad is also important. When the centre of the pad is high, mental powers rule. Set low, they will be practical, but if centrally placed, their talents will be interpreted in a more balanced fashion.

Irrespective of whether the hand is soft or firm, there will be a lack of physical stamina, but this does not mean poor health. These types really are not suited to a strenuous business life. Nor are they known for their sporting triumphs. They enjoy sport – from an

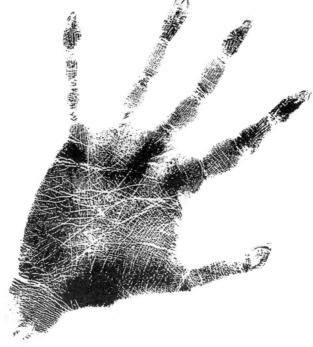

Note the long, slim fingers, the curve at the
percussion and many lines associated with this type of hand.

35

armchair, no doubt – and can be very knowledgeable, but are not actively involved.

They are likely to be found supporting or following genteel affairs like gymkhanas or other similar country affairs. Such people will not be found on the terraces at a football or rugby game, but may be in the crowd at a cricket match.

These individuals are not practical, for theirs is a world of inspiration and idealism. They exist more in a dream-land on an emotional, psychic or mental plane.

Poets, lovers and others of yester-year enthused much over these hands in their poems and sonnets when they spoke in such glowing terms of the pale hands of their amours. As poets, they may well have been in love, but had little knowledge of palmistry!

Of all the other hand shapes, perhaps only the conic hand has any rapport with them, for they both dream a lot. But at least conic-handed types try to make something of their ideals.

Those with square and spatulate hands cannot identify with them at all, while folk with the philosophical hand shape do not even bother to try. There is no mutual attraction, simply nothing to appeal to either type at all. Thus, it is usually only a matter of time before all pointed-hand types naturally gravitate together. If they do not, they could be doomed to spend much of their time in a kind of isolation.

One writer on hands claimed the psychic hand type is composed of "flame and light" while all of the others are made of "flesh and blood". Pointed hand shapes were – and still are – to be found more in the oriental world where the history and legends of old originated.

Many hundreds of years ago, people with these shaped hands were prominent in the ruling classes. Inter-breeding and the gradual loss of practical and mundane matters – like fighting skills or science and diplomatic techniques, such as they were then – lost them their temporal power.

However, despite this, they are not perfect souls either, for they are just as prone to temptation as the rest of us, but fight battles in their minds for too long and neglect what they consider are unimportant or minor matters.

This leads others to feel they are more unreliable than most, for if they are unable to solve a problem, they walk away from it. If the impulse takes them, they forget their mundane obligations and concentrate on any new matters to the exclusion of all else.

With this hand, the palmar surface will be covered in a multitude of lines and influence marks running here and there all over it – the "full" hand. The mind is never still. This means that the subject finds it difficult to switch off, to rest when he is supposed to.

A firm hand and a fairly strong thumb helps a dedicated few to become actors and actresses of a very special calibre. He or she can immerse themselves so totally in a character, we tend to admire or remember them more for the part than for themselves.

When there is a very firm pointed hand, these folk are likely to turn to other modes of entertaining. They make excellent stage magicians or illusionists, and excel as speciality balancing artistes or jugglers, for there is always a keen sense of balance.

However, because they are not as materialistic as other hand shapes, they are much more likely to work caring for others.

There is almost always a gift for persuasive oratory with a first-class command of language. But, first and foremost, they are idealists, and as is so often the case, they have little idea of what is going on around them until it is too late.

7

The Elementary or Basic Hand

It is absolutely essential to remember that although this hand looks short, stubby and even clumsy, it does not follow that the subject's personality will reflect these qualities. Often, people with this hand have far more going for them than those who completed a university education.

However, it is fair to say that this hand does not exactly impress with its heavy, short, stubby fingers, an equally short and stubby thumb that looks as if it was put on as an afterthought, and often badly-bitten nails.

More often than not, the hand looks weather-beaten and heavily tanned from outdoor pursuits. It is rarely pale and uninteresting. Often wider than it is long, when it comes to the lines, only the three principal lines of head, heart and life are present and very little else.

However, a closer examination will show a well-proportioned and surprisingly long head line. Of course, while there will always be a few small influence lines crossing here and there, this is without doubt the best example of the "empty" hand.

The knuckles and joints of the fingers are not always prominent, and might even seem to be smooth and almost lost in the overall thick appearance of the hand as a whole. The "mouse", the health mount at the back of the hand between the thumb and first finger, is always full and firm to the touch.

The skin pattern tends to be "wide" and heavy-looking, and quite easily seen with the naked eye. This is very useful when taking prints because the patterns on the fingers and palms will be clearly reproduced.

Because this hand is stiff and apparently inflexible, it should not be taken to mean the owner has an unyielding personality, or is slow to think or act. Although this may be true up to a point, if the thinking is slow it could be due to habit.

The rather wide palm and fingers are virtually the same length.
The thumb is small for the hand.

People like this leave alone things they do not understand. In turn, this leads to many misunderstandings. Those with this hand shape are not fools. In fact, they are quite the reverse, being gifted with a good feel for – and a knowledge of – nature.

Their instinctive approach to life and its problems is basically honest. They know what is right and wrong. For the most part, their world is uncomplicated and full of common-sense.

There is little interest in anything intellectual, for they much prefer to keep things plain and straightforward. The old adage of calling a spade a spade makes a lot of sense to these people, but does not mean they lack intelligence.

A quick appraisal of their head line will disprove the point, for as a rule it will be far better developed and etched than those found on other hand shapes. Meanwhile, a palm with long fingers always indicates basic manual skills.

While it is said that these folk lack imagination and subtlety, they certainly make up for it with a sound, common sense approach. They are creatures of routine who seem to have given up on any effort or simply let the world pass them by. They are also hard and fast realists.

Able to put up with almost any hardship, fatalistic and resigned, they become used to a tough way of life as a matter of course, an environment to which they have become accustomed. However, these people have certain gifts for which others might give their right arm.

They have a way with animals, flowers and plants. Routine matters are instinctively attended to, with little desire to break out of this way of life. There is little or no inclination for the culture, refinement or intellectual advancement knowledge can bring.

Broadly speaking, on a hand like this, the line of life is quite heavily etched into the palmar surface. In the majority of cases, it starts faintly, lightly tied to the line of head, sweeps out in the palm and continues strongly all the way to the base of the palm.

It mostly tucks in under the thumb, indicating a love of the comforts of home with little inclination for travel. The line can end on the mount of Neptune, which reflects an affinity with all things natural. This is an intuitive, instinctive approach to life few outsiders appreciate or understand. Should the line end on the mount of the Moon, travel aspirations might be limited to watching television programmes about holidays and such like.

The line of head is often clear, long and well-marked, and implies good, sensible imaginative powers. As a rule, they will be straightforward, honest and mean well, but there is always a sense of mischief lurking behind their knowing eyes.

Generally, the line of heart is set low on the palm and tends to run straight across the hand. It usually starts between the mounts of Jupiter and Saturn, with a fairly wide space between it and the line of heart.

This shows plain, old-fashioned commonsense and practicality. When anything does faze them, they soon sort out what is wrong in their own inimitable style. Because there are so few other lines, they have an objective outlook.

Their temper is quick to rise, slow to fall, and the memory long. It does not pay to make an enemy of this person because, if he so chooses, he will run rings around you to your personal discomfort and embarrassment, especially with witnesses present.

You will not find these people among our world leaders, but you cannot do without them, either. Someone has to give the orders … and someone has to do the work!

With their wide palms, sound constitution, physical strength and down-to-earth approach they are just as clever as everyone else, and more so in some cases. Think for a moment and remember when you once stood and watched a workman lay a brick wall or pipes, or a farmer plough a furrow, and did not envy them their skills. The ancient Chinese palmists were so right when they called this "the hand of the earth".

8
The Mixed Hand

Until now we have studied the pure type of the traditional hand shapes. Of course, I must also point out that apart from the square or conic hand, pure types are rarely encountered.

The mixed hand cannot be a pure type because there are so many variations. As a result, it is easily the most misunderstood and certainly the most complex of them all.

Mixed hands are confusing as they do not conform to any of the other classifications, although they might possibly be mistaken for an extreme version of any one of them, but only up to a point.

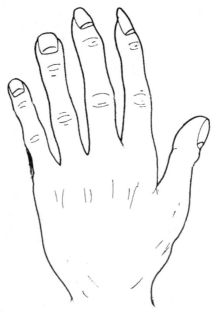

A print cannot properly show the features of a mixed hand, so the differing fingertips have been deliberately exaggerated to do so.

The palm may be neither square nor conic: there might be a partly developed creative curve on the outer edge of the hand or it will be quite straight. Sometimes, it seems like the ideal or psychic hand while at other times it may be partly spatulate at the top or bottom of the palm.

Then there are the fingers to take into account. With knotting on some of the fingers, it might be mistaken for the philosophic type. The index finger is often one shape, the middle another, the third and fourth different yet again. The permutations are many. And if you also take into account long and short fingers, soft and hard textures, stiff or yielding hands, these variations become legion.

The golden rule is to observe. When the hand does not comply with the usual requirements and the fingers are as different as I have just outlined, then accept the hand for what it is – a mixture.

Prints cannot do this hand justice. Nor can a good photograph. The physical hand has to be studied to understand it fully. The illustration for this hand has been specially exaggerated. At first sight, it may seem square, then the curve at the outer edge makes you feel it is conic.

Each of the tips are different. The index finger is pointed, but the middle knotted at both joints, suggesting the philosophic type. There is a spatulated tip on the third finger while the fourth finger is basically square. The thumb is rather heavy, with a slightly bulbous tip, and at the base there is an angle of time. Each of the fingers are evenly set on the top of the palm.

Always remember that no matter what the individual parts of a mixed hand suggest, the owners are adaptable. Changeable, always on the look-out for new ideas and interests, they are restless and versatile, but inconsistent and volatile if you catch them at the wrong moment.

Responsive and always ready to take a chance, these folk attempt anything once – and again if they like it. For them, challenge is the accepted norm.

A hidebound, red tape, petty bureaucratic life is not for them. Their personal motto might read, "I want – and I shall have!" They do live life to the full.

However, they have their weaknesses. For a start, there is a lazy streak second to none. No matter how hard a hand may feel to the touch, this seems to be an inbuilt mixed-hand trait for all. These folk work in fits and starts, but when they work, they really do work!

They also play as hard. Many have a gambling streak. This may not be restricted to monetary matters, but also to life. The mixed hand frequently has short middle fingers but long third fingers, the classic sign of a gambling nature. When the first finger is also short – or at least shorter than the third finger – this trait is emphasised.

These people adapt as they experience life. Some learn from their mistakes, others never do. Behaviour patterns are conditioned by the individual development or otherwise of each part of the hand.

A palmist has to learn quickly to be very careful when he comes to analyse the mixed hand personality. It is best to start with the thumb. It needs to be well-shaped and firm. In some cases, it may be slightly heavy for the hand upon which it is found. But this is good, for it goes a long way to ensure that the willpower indicated ought to be properly used.

As far as the lines are concerned, the head line has to have sufficient development to be resourceful enough for the varying activities with which these personalities are most likely to be involved.

Further, those with mixed hands have a rather selfish nature and are much inclined to look after number one to the exclusion of all others all of the time, especially if the basic shape is a mixture of the conic and elementary types. Power, ambition and possession are very strong driving forces.

For those with firm hands and large thumbs, the pursuit of wealth, status and position is always strong. Very little is allowed to get in their way as they strive for these achievements.

If the philosophic and square hands appear to have joined forces, the subject will be fascinated by abstract science. Rather difficult to live with, they are best left to their own devices. Emotional considerations are not a strong point at all. In fact, the needs and wants of a close partner can often be overlooked, and are probably the last things they think about.

If there is a mix of the psychic and conic shapes, a much more emotional but peaceful character will be evident. These people live in a world of their own. If everything is peaceful and quiet, they get along with just about anyone as long as they keep to their side of any bargain.

Regrettably, these types do not last long in this modern world: the hustle and bustle are too much for them so they tend to live in small, close-knit communities with their own kind, rather like escapists.

However, irrespective of this basic foundation, mixed-hand types can work equally well together, or as part of a team. If on their own, they set their own pace: with others, they find their niche and stay there.

When they marry or enter any long-term association, such characters will try to make it last or shy away from the idea altogether. It is one way or the other, with few half measures here. Many never seem to stay long enough in one place to become attached to someone else anyway.

Quite probably, it was somebody with mixed hands who popularised this now modern trend of a man and woman living together and made it socially acceptable. If nothing else, these mixed-hand types are practical!

They are among the best and most successful small-business people. These individuals thrive well in a local market wheeling and dealing on a stall, or in small local premises, perhaps employing about a dozen or so people. Mostly, they make an honest living and are respected for the way they deal with others.

Generally speaking, they are open and fair, but it does not pay to confide too much about future plans to them. They are very shrewd – and if they can get in first, they also know how to profit from it!

Whatever their faults – and they have a few – the ability to succeed and shine at whatever they do is always there. There is an inbuilt determination to win through, perhaps more so than in any of the other shapes put together.

9

Fire, Earth, Air and Water Hands

Each of the seven traditional basic shapes – the square; conic, or round; spatulate; elementary; psychic; philosophic; the mixed – and their associated meanings have been fully discussed.

These more modern ideas were first discussed around 40–50 years ago. This method of classifying hands follows the principles of the four elements: fire, earth, air and water.

This simplifies the classification from seven shapes to only four. While it is much easier to recognise only four categories, it is rather purist for those who pursue the traditional ways.

To condense seven into four seems a hard task at first sight, but that is not what happens. This new ideology goes back to basics and starts all over again. Those new to the study often make the mistake of trying to cross-reference between the old and the new. It just does not work … and is wrong to try. Although the terminology is the same, that is where it ends.

To decide to which of these groups your hands belong, look at them to see if your palm is basically square or rectangular, irrespective of the creative curve that might or might not be present.

Next, look at your fingers and decide if they are long or short in comparison to the palm. Fingers should be accepted as long if the middle finger is as long or longer than the palm measured from the wrist to the base of the middle finger. They are considered as short if the finger of Saturn is less than this. Using this system, your hand will fall into one of the following four types.

If you have a rectangular palm with short fingers, it is a Fire hand. Should you possess a rectangular palm with long fingers, then your hand belongs to the Water hand group. When your palm appears to be square with short fingers, you have an Earth hand. If your palm is square with long fingers, you belong to the Air hand group.

Individual finger and tip shapes retain traditional associations, so if your hand belongs to the water type your long fingers can still be classified as square, round, spatulate or pointed.

The Fire Hand

Basically, this is a rectangular hand with fingers shorter than the palm. The fingers may be slightly wider at their tips, not exactly spatulate, but near so.

This shape indicates an extrovert approach to life – enthusiastic, enterprising and intelligent folk who make natural leaders, and are at their best when organising people and things.

Man-management is a second nature, for there is an instinctive or inbuilt ability to motivate and inspire others with their natural zeal. Always full of ideas and rarely still for long because they have to be doing something, they need to keep their hands and minds occupied.

With their infectious personality, they easily persuade others to their way of thinking. Social leaders and rarely followers, there is such a natural flair for taking charge it is almost second nature to them.

These people are fond of sport and most outdoor activities. They are the life and soul of any gathering, formal or otherwise. Despite this, they also have an inbuilt self-destruct mode – a lazy streak second to none. It is always best, therefore, to have a capable second-in-command waiting to take over if this happens, or all their good work just disappears down the nearest drain.

Sometimes, it is as though they are unable to monitor their natural reserves. They either burn themselves out or ruin things in a senseless act of crass stupidity. It is the deputy who carries out what the Fire hand directs.

The Earth Hand

These people are the salt of the earth, solid, down-to-earth and level-headed folk who do not stand for any nonsense from anyone.

Very much creatures of routine, conventional, law-abiding, rather pragmatic and traditional in outlook, they are always reliable. Mostly neat and tidy, with a place for everything and everything in its place, they are so clever and creative with their hands.

Outdoor pursuits attract, and with their great love for animals, large or small, they are close to nature. Such individuals flourish best working with animals or with their hands as carpenters, gardeners or metal workers, or on the land. Because they cope so well with routine, they do well in the armed forces, the police or security work. They have a lot of patience for detailed work.

These folk also have a knack for being able to instruct. They do not teach as such. Rather, they have a special gift for being able to school recruits in the ways of the organisation to which they now belong.

They can be impatient and abrupt, especially when people or plans fail to do what they should. And if you make a mistake they will reduce you to about six inches high as they tell you exactly what they think of you. Loyal employees and as honest as they come, they have a good sense of responsibility.

The Air Hand

This hand is flexible and quite supple, which indicates a receptive and understanding character and personality. Mental pursuits and subjects like languages or modern communication technology such as computers attract.

This is what they need to keep them occupied, for the stimulus of change and variety is essential to their well-being. In some very special cases, it is not unknown for them to vary their journey to work each day just to keep their spirits up, for they tend to have a very low boredom threshold. Thus, travel obviously attracts as it is another form of communication.

Journalism, photography, the media generally and courier work all attract people with the Air hand. The entertainment industry is full of individuals like these because they have mercurial minds. They are almost unflappable, and know how to turn disadvantage to their advantage very quickly indeed.

Their personal life can be changeable because they seem to control their emotional nature. They approach a problem logically rather than with emotion. It is so easy for them to miss out on the joy and pain of love and romance. To those who do not know them very well, they can appear cool or distant.

The Water Hand

This type is too emotional. They respond to atmosphere, mood and colour too easily. Moody and predictably unpredictable, they are also ultra-sensitive and often very highly strung. Because of this, they become quite vulnerable to bullies and other insensitive types, especially in the early days when still at school.

They really do need to keep both feet very firmly on the ground because they get so caught up with everything. For example, when a new romance knocks their feet out from under them, it can send them totally into a world all of their own. Often, they fall in love with love rather than the new object of their affections.

This group does well in the caring professions for they can empathise. They listen and speak well, and spend many hours simply listening to those who need an ear or constant care. They love the creative arts and are frequently found in the ranks of artists, musicians and writers.

Equally, anything in the health and beauty industry suits them, for they understand, manipulate and influence trends that operate in this world. While they may not do too well in mundane affairs because they respond far too readily to changes of atmosphere and moods, they can still be very perceptive and shrewd in their dealings.

Perhaps it is because their own moods swing either way so readily that they are much better off in this kind of creative atmosphere where their sensibilities can be gainfully employed.

10
The Back of the Hands

When you first start to look at people's hands, no matter where you are or who you are with, you have to begin somewhere. More often than not, you find yourself staring at the back of a pair of hands wondering just where and how you do begin.

If possible, try noting if someone is left-handed or not, how they hold a pen or pencil, or a knife, fork or spoon. If they smoke, notice how they hold their cigar, cigarette or pipe, and watch how they dispose of the ash.

Observe how people hold a cup, glass, plate or drinking glass. Look for those little personal gestures not just of the whole hand, but also the smaller, intimate movements of fingers and thumbs either towards themselves or with those near and dear.

Look to see if they wear a ring or rings, and on what finger or fingers. Do they bite, nibble or paint their nails? A biter is worse than a nibbler as their temper is usually less controlled. A nibbler may be only temporarily worried. Painted nails can hide a multitude of sins.

A bus or train ride now becomes quite an adventure, full of fun as you read people rather than a book, magazine or newspaper. This exercise is, of course, a one-sided affair, but any covert observation is not only entertaining, it is also educational, too.

Just occasionally, especially in very special circumstances, it is perfectly proper politely to ask the person under scrutiny a question about a feature of their character or personality with which you may be uncertain from simple observation.

As a rule, most will be only too pleased to help and chat with you because they can then talk about themselves – and the majority of people love to do that! It is like winding up a clock because once they are in full flow about their favourite subject, there is no stopping them and you will have a wonderful opportunity to study their hands without any hindrance at all.

Look, learn, listen and observe. But be warned: it is not always that easy, especially when you meet someone for the first time. A person with short fingers and long palms or just small hands, for instance, will want to hear short, precise answers to their questions and wave away long or detailed explanations. But people who have large hands require detailed explanations and will want to consider all the possibilities before a reply is given.

Those with rather small or narrow hands may be selfish, but this is not always apparent on a first meeting. They are opportunists who can move very quickly indeed to secure an advantage. People with this type of hand need careful watching and understanding.

Long, narrow hands show someone who takes time to think things through before they commit themselves. When the fingers look as though they have a bulge or knotting at each of the joints, he or she will be a deeply philosophic type.

Large hands, those which are wide across the back of the palm, belong to someone who will not stand for any nonsense. Big hands can make a person appear physically larger than he is. This does not mean he is slow in perception or action, but is a materialist. Meanwhile, large, broad hands indicate an individual who likes the great outdoors.

When the skin looks sunburned, weather-beaten or feels rough, all kinds of outdoor pursuits attract. Here, the subject may be the type of craftsman who prefers to work outdoors, especially if his hands are square.

Whereas a wide back to the hand suggests a love of outdoor life, the narrow, smooth or pale hand with a soft texture indicates a preference for indoor life. A slight tan is to be expected in hot, sunny times, usually as a result of people indulging their lazy streak by simply sitting out in the sun. As a rule, with these characters, other sports or similar pursuits are indulged from the comfort of an armchair in front of their television.

Hair on the hands and fingers, together with the texture of the skin, also gives clues to character, but these may be more as a guide than definite statements of fact.

Hairiness suggests a sound constitution but not physical strength, which is a very old, traditional suggestion now proven incorrect. A dead-white hand which gives the appearance of pallor or a lack of blood (not one which is white on account of fineness), reveals a nature that lacks the normal enthusiasm and passion for life.

Cold by nature, people with pale hands shy away from an active social life and may often appear distant or do not seem to make much of an effort to please others, even those near and dear. Equally, they rarely show much sympathy when things go wrong for other people, but these folk do not seek much or expect anything for themselves when things do not go well with them.

Blue or purplish hands are usually a sign of bad circulation with attendant poor blood pressure, perhaps localised rather than an overall matter. As we grow older, reaction to heat and cold becomes restricted. The hands and feet are often the first to feel the difference.

People with red hands enjoy good health. Full of enthusiasm and energy most of the time, they are purposeful and unable to do anything by halves.

Large hands suggest the owners are slow to anger, but when their temper is aroused they become quite violent. It is difficult for them to exercise self-control.

Sometimes, there may be an obvious difference between two hands other than those caused by accident or illness. Once seen, it is never forgotten. When the right hand seems more positive-looking than the left and shows signs of being distinctly stronger, the subject will have made definite efforts to better himself. When the left hand is so obviously much stronger-looking, the owner could have suffered a major set-back from which it may have been difficult to recover.

Alternatively, it could be an indication that the subject is a drifter who has slipped into an easy way of life. To find out how much of this is just a passing phase, take a closer look at the rest of the hand and, of course, the lines for more supportive evidence.

When faced with two distinctly different hands, for example, when the right is clearly conic but the left obviously square, check for the consistency of the hands. When the right hand is firmer than the left, it suggests that the conic hand's more overt tendencies tend to dominate the natural conservatism of the square hand.

The extrovert approach implied by the conic hand, its creativity, love of the artistic world and overall sense of fun is replaced with the subject's practical and orthodox outlook. When the left hand is firmer, these indications are reversed.

There could be several reasons for this anomaly. Often, it may be as a result of the influence of both parents, especially in the formative years. They might well have come from very different backgrounds or be quite different in personality and character. This situation causes the subject to have difficulty in coming to terms with what is basically a three-fold type of relationship.

In dealing with these deeply emotional and often stressful times, the subject will have compromised and adopted two quite different poses more or less continuously to come to terms with a difficult situation. A quick check on the palmar side will confirm this.

When there is a knotting or bulging at the finger joints, the owner will be reasonably orderly and methodical. If all the lower phalanges, those at the base of the fingers, are pronounced, then the owners are basically materialistic. They may be quite careless and untidy in their immediate surroundings, at home or in their work-place, but are tidy in personal appearance.

A careful survey of the knuckles yields useful information. If the first finger knuckle is more pronounced than the others, a great deal of personal pride, a love of ritual and a sense of tradition and love of country will be evident.

When the second knuckle is the most prominent, it shows a strong love of order and neatness in the personal life and environment. An emphasised third finger knuckle indicates a flair for giving things an extra special touch that many others find impossible to achieve even with a lot of effort.

When the knuckle on the little finger is prominent, the subject displays an instinctive approach to all forms of tidiness. In the business world especially, it shows someone fully conversant with modern commercial organisation and methods.

When you look at the back of a hand you cannot help but note the nails. Although we shall deal with them in more detail later, a couple of guidelines will help you with an initial assessment.

Generally speaking, people with large nails have a more peaceful, balanced and expansive attitude to life than do those with small nails. Small nails imply a critical nature and a more restricted approach to life.

If there is a wide gap between the end of the nails and the tips of the finger, the owner will have a hasty and explosive temper. He is likely to blow up if he cannot have his own way, and is not known for diplomacy. Generally, however, any display of bad temper is over almost as soon as it starts.

It takes time and effort to become proficient, and then only when you practise. Always make time to look at the hands of everyone with whom you come into contact.

11
The Nails

When we look at someone else's hands, especially the backs, we tend to notice the nails first. As a rule, the eyes are drawn to the nails because of their appearance, particularly so if they are badly kept, well maintained or, of course, painted with nail-varnish in such a way that they are noticeable.

Nails are very important. For one thing, they indicate the current state of health and temperament of the individual. In a clinical sense, a quick examination of the nails is quite likely to reveal certain types of mineral deficiency, nervous tension, physical or mental well-being, stress and, sometimes, vascular problems. As far as temperament is concerned, nails show whether a person has a short, sharp temper, is critical, superficially charming or fairly placid.

THE TEN MOST COMMONLY ENCOUNTERED NAIL SHAPES

*From left to right: (Top line) short, rectangular, filbert, almond, wide
(Bottom line) narrow, shell, talon, dished, curved.*

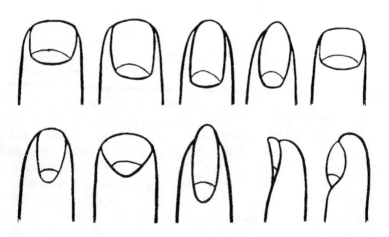

Physically, a nail is composed of horn and takes about six months to grow from the hidden root. It is a continual growth process. Any indentation, mark or scar made at the base of the nail will take about 180 days to grow out.

This does not apply to the small horizontal barring that appears as a result of illness. Nor does it apply to the longitudinal ridging which often appears, perhaps more so in bitten nails, which are always a strong indication that the nervous system is under stress or strain.

Any nail that shows a sign of horizontal barring and longitudinal ridges together indicates poor health through organic, glandular or endocrine imbalance. This, in turn, has an effect on the overall nervous disposition. As a rule, this will more than likely result in irritability and tiredness. There will be a feeling of being run-down.

When white specks are found on any part of the nail, it suggests certain mineral deficiencies and, if also located on bitten nails, poor emotional balance and signs of irritability, or an inherent chronic psychological problem.

Using the formula set out earlier, it is quite possible to date the onset of this current bout of ill-health. When the markings are halfway along the nail, it suggests problems started about three months earlier.

If there are both horizontal and longitudinal ridging, check the palmar side of the hand. The lines could show the probable cause as an emotional shock, an infection, nutritional imbalance or accident.

Each nail should have a clear half-moon at its base, which is a good sign of a healthy body and a contented, inner disposition. If no moons are to be seen, it suggests a weak constitution at that time. Moons can and do suddenly disappear, a sure sign of an impending temporary illness. When there are no moons to be seen, you should ask if this has always been the case. The nails may be indicating a temporary period of ill-health.

A nice, pale, milky pink is the best colour for nails because it implies a reasonably placid disposition. Deeper than this shows a temperament easily aroused. Pale nails indicate possible anaemia while the white nail characterises a cold or selfish nature.

A yellowish tinge or spotting on the nail might imply a kidney or liver disorder. Irrespective of colour, nails should have a nice, natural lustre to them. Where this is not the case, there may be a loss of trace elements.

When white spots are seen *on* the nail, not any white flecking *in* the nail, word your advice carefully. These spots are often known to get sufficiently serious enough to make the nail brittle. It could be a form of demineralisation and require treatment.

Personality and Character in the Nail

Palmists often differ when it comes to the interpretation of nails. There are some rather different modern ideas currently in vogue, though perhaps not yet fully proven. It is best – and safest – to adopt a traditional approach. The following interpretations are traditional and the most reliable.

There are only four basic nail shapes: broad or narrow, long or short, and a number of variations. This list is limited to the ten most commonly seen nails. If, or when, you see a nail that does not quite conform, adapt the meaning of the one nearest in description to it.

People with nails wider than they are long are quick to anger and equally quick to forget. Impulsive, forthright and critical in word and deed, they are reasonably resilient and their health is sound. As a rule, they are not prone to catching any bug currently going the rounds in their environment.

Narrow nails imply a rather delicate constitution or, perhaps, a lack of physical energy. The owner may well make up for this with more than his or her share of nervous energy. Often, this nail will have fluting – longitudinal ridging – or show a slight blue tinge near the moon. This suggests a certain amount of vascular weakness, but nothing to worry about.

People with a long, square or rectangular nail have a nature slow to anger, and are mostly placid and reasonably settled. When those with this nail are upset, they do eventually forgive, but it is quite rare for them to forget. Diet, health and hygiene matters are a strong point. They are somewhat fastidious and do not like to get their hands dirty.

The short, square nail always indicates a critical nature. There seems to be a lack of warmth, and the character may lack feeling. The owner is physically active, but likely to have a restricted or restrictive emotional or mental outlook on life.

The shell-like nail suggests physical and emotional ill-health, ultra-sensitivity, and a generally run-down state that can often occur after a sudden shock to the system. People with this nail must take things easy, slow down and ease back. This character tends to be impulsive, hasty and ready to jump to conclusions.

The talon-shaped nail reflects a poor or inadequate diet, which in turn reflects a lowered state of health. In manner, such folk tend to be somewhat superficial, cold and distant, even calculating at times, those with little or no finesse at all. In addition, there will be some selfishness: this one is a born survivor.

Almond nails reflect a steady, aesthetic, refined character and personality. Devoted to anyone who shows them a little affection, they are honest, loyal, and truthful friends. Little really fazes them, but they are known to display nervous, almost uncontrollable hysterical outbursts when upset.

People with filbert nails are generally peace-loving, placid and fairly slow to anger. They often live on their nervous energy much more than is good for them. There is a lazy streak. If upset, they are likely to go off and sulk for ages, like a recalcitrant child. They tend not to show anger in the physical sense, but may become slightly hysterical or a tad out of control for a few moments.

Dished nails suggest health problems affecting glands, perhaps a poor blood supply or nutritional deficiency. The dishing effect occurs because of nervous or emotional stress and seems to affect the weakest part of the body. These subjects are often dull or listless, with quirky inconsistencies of temperament.

The bulbous, curved nail (the Hippocratic nail), is a symptom of chest or respiratory problems. It is medically recognised as a symptom of smoking. The nature is selfish and inclined to hedonism, for these people are prepared to try almost anything in their pursuit of pleasure.

12
The Fingers

A study of the fingers always shows a lot about the character and personality of the individual, for where fingers reveal our instinctive attitudes, the palm represents our outward and more practical side. Thus, the overall appearance, development and shape of each finger taken individually or collectively are very strong indications of character in their own right.

The fingers need to be examined from both the front and back because it is necessary to study their relationships to each other, their neighbours and other parts of the hand. Equally, you must also compare the fingers of both hands to each other. The classification of the fingertips will be dealt with elsewhere.

Finger length
At first, measurement of the fingers can be difficult for those new to the study. To establish whether fingers are long or short, take a ruler and measure the middle finger from its tip to where it joins the top of the hand.

Next, measure down the palm from this upper point to where the hand joins the wrist. This could be one of several places – from where the skin patterns fade out, or where the upper bracelet, or rascette, crosses the wrist at the base of the palm. If the middle finger is shorter than the palm, then the fingers must be classified as short. When the medius is longer than the palm, the fingers should be classified overall as long.

It is rare for this middle finger to be shorter than any of the others, but if so, then measure the longest finger, which is almost certainly bound to be the third or Apollo finger.

Finger set
The way each of the fingers are set on the top of the palm is of great

importance. Basically, there are four principal types and they may be likened to styles of architectural arches.

The most predominant is when they appear set like a Norman arch, the central pivot at the base of the middle finger. The index and little fingers are more low-set than the others. If they are set very low, they seem to form a Perpendicular arch.

A low-set first finger reflects a lack of self-confidence. If very low, the owner displays little push or initiative, and the personality is flat, dull and uninteresting.

Expect to find signs of an inferiority complex when both little fingers are low-set. The owners dislike becoming involved in an active social life. They do not trust anyone very much … and that includes relatives or long-standing family friends. In addition, there may be problems expressing their emotional needs properly, especially when the fourth finger is very low set.

When the fingers are evenly set along the top of the palm like a Tudor arch, the subject tends to have a well-balanced personality, someone who can ride with the rough and the smooth equally well. He trusts his own judgement and has a positive outlook, with all the necessary self-assuredness needed to succeed.

The fourth group is illustrated when the fingers slope down from a high-set Jupiter finger to a low-set Mercury. Here the subject seems to experience what others might feel is a misplaced self-confidence, for these folk will try to carry all before them in one big bluff when all else fails.

But this charade is exposed at the first challenge when their world crumbles about them like a pack of cards. When this happens, more often than not, the fingers are quite short, which accentuates impulsive actions.

Smooth fingers

Where the fingers are smooth, without any indication of bulging or knotting at the joints, the subject tends to be quick-witted and perceptive. Should knots be present at the joints, it is as if they act as a dam or weir and hold back the free flow of ideas.

With smooth fingers, there is nothing to stop this inward flow of information: the brain is able to digest and decide much quicker.

Smooth fingers show versatility and an intuitive character. If smooth and short, there will be an impulsive streak, people who know instinctively what is expected of them. However, they are likely to accept a task without completely appreciating all the details it may entail, and off they go to where angels would never venture. Detail is just not their forte. Further, these people have a habit of committing themselves to a task they have not a hope of completing and overload themselves with responsibilities often far beyond their capabilities.

Spontaneous, well-meaning and always among the first to offer help, if they cannot fully grasp what they are about to tackle, the whole affair is doomed to failure.

People with long, smooth fingers are the opposite. Such individuals thrive on intricacy and detail. They stop, look and listen, consider what is needed and take the necessary action. An impulsive nature is still present, but it is curbed. They are still adaptable, quick and versatile, but not nearly as much as those with short fingers.

Knotted fingers

A knot, or emphasis at any of the phalangeal joints, should be seen as acting as a temporary stop or check on the inward flow of information. A critical nature will be evident. This is someone who has to examine everything first before making a decision or taking action – irrespective of the shape of the fingertips.

Knots at the first or top joints suggest a personality who is slow and difficult to please, one who worries unnecessarily and becomes a victim to inner nervous tension as a result.

When it comes to moments of real importance, like a promotional or new job interview, for example, they often give a poor showing and fail. This is despite having an excellent knowledge of what is expected of them.

If the lower joints are knotted, it indicates a pragmatic, rather basic and methodical character. Neat, tidy and orderly all the time, these types also dress in a conservative fashion. This is carried over into their views on life as well. Personal discipline will always be apparent as such folk favour traditionalism.

The mark of the true sceptic is when both joints are prominent. Expect to find a concise, cold and cutting nature, characters who can be so obsessively neat and tidy in everything they do.

There is little room for any emotional consideration when there is a decision to be made. Extremely logical at all times, if an action has to be taken, they take it. Often, they have more than one interest on the go at any one time. If their attention palls, they move on to another as their mood or concentration level changes.

Difficult to please, they prefer quiet, studious surroundings. They are well-suited to research work because it enables them to blend a love of practicality with their intellectual prowess.

The knuckles

Strictly speaking, knuckles are the third finger joints. Any development here will be reflected in personal appearance, and health and hygiene matters. If they all look fairly even, the owner demonstrates the gift of always looking neat and tidy no matter what they wear or are doing at the time. It would be rare to see a man without his tie, or the woman in her slippers or curlers. A major weakness is over-concern with diet and personal discipline. In some cases, they are out-and-out food faddists.

Uneven knuckles show an outward concern with orderliness, but this is just superficial. In such cases, the middle finger knuckle is the most prominent, in which case the owner pays only lip service to his personal habits, hygiene, appearance and possessions. His or her rooms may look neat and tidy, but when you open a drawer or lift a cushion the true decline of their character is likely to show.

These are the people who exhibit such a pantomime as they search through their pockets or purses for keys, matches or money.

Finger spacing

It is easy to assess spacing between the fingers because they are either wide or narrow. Check both hands, for fingers can have wide spacing between them on one hand while the other has quite narrow spacing.

Fingers may turn inward and look like claws, or open outward and seem quite supple.

Wide spacing

An obvious gap between the first and second fingers shows a good level of self-confidence with an added love of independence. These people tend not to be one of the herd and go to a lot of trouble to maintain their independence.

This is the sure mark of a manager, but not necessarily a leader. This one controls, directs and carries out the instructions of those who are higher up the ladder. He or she functions best when decisions have to be made, for they instinctively know how to act and, more to the point, when.

If a wide space is found between the middle and ring fingers, it highlights a resourceful but selfishly inclined character. There is a lack of thought where others are concerned. Their long-term planning is not exactly a strong point, so they tend to exist more on a day-to-day basis, frequently playing everything by ear.

Sometimes, wide spacing here can signify shyness or reticence in social affairs. Privacy is essential, especially when they have to find time to recharge their batteries. They guard their space zealously.

Wide spacing between the third and fourth fingers shows individuals with a preference for acting independently. They prize a lone-wolf kind of independence, and are not one of the herd at all. Physical restriction of any kind is anathema to them. They get along well on their own and it helps them retain their sense of identity.

They must be free to act as and when they want, and provided you respect this, they will be happy to co-operate with you. There is an intense dislike of vacillation. If something has to be done, let it be done.

When the fingers and thumbs all have wide spaces between them, the nature is extrovert and individual. Freedom of thought is highly valued because, as a rule, they are open and frank, always ready to express their thoughts and criticism.

Narrow Spaces

When the space between the index and middle fingers is narrow, the owners prefer to go along with the crowd no matter what personal feelings are experienced. They lack confidence, with a little too much dependency on others than is good for them. They have a need for constant reassurance to keep going.

When there is a narrow space between the middle and ring fingers, the owner is always mindful of the immediate and distant future. Personal security is essential as is planning for the future. He or she does not like to take chances with anything.

If there is a narrow space between the third and fourth fingers, it suggests too much dependency on others. These people feel better as part of the herd because for them safety in numbers is most reassuring. Their best place is in the middle of a crowd.

When the gaps between all the fingers and thumbs are narrow, the owner has a closed mind. He or she is very dependent on others. They go along with the mood of the moment at all times. It is rare for them to question the motives of others.

Flexibility

More properly to detect flexibility of the hand and fingers, you have to do so physically. There is no harm in asking the subject to help by carrying out little exercises at your direction.

You should test the fingers in the same way as the thumb is appraised. Their individual and collective flexibility will indicate quite different character traits to those shown by a set of stiff and unyielding fingers.

Flexible fingers indicate a flexible mind, a pleasant nature, one eager to please and who gets along with everyone, However, if the fingers are stiff or unyielding, the nature is unyielding, stiff, formal and a trifle selfish.

The ability to bend the fingers backward between the top and the second phalange shows an innate natural intuition for receiving and acting on new information. The mind is receptive and reacts intuitively on all messages received.

However, if the fingers are stiff and unbending, the owner is more likely to be conservative, with a very conventional outlook. When the fingers are collectively flexible between the middle and base phalanges, it shows someone with a fair share of common sense and practicality.

If the nail phalange is the longest, there is an intellectual basis behind all they do. A decision will have to be made to see if a project is worth doing. But if the basal phalanges are the longest, these people are able to turn their hands to just about anything because when given the opportunity, working with their hands is second nature.

When all the fingers readily bend backward at the knuckles, he or she will be impressionable, willing to do the bidding of others, a follower rather than a leader, perhaps slightly unreliable, someone who is certainly not pushy.

A reasonably flexible hand at the knuckles shows the owner to be adaptable, one who acts quickly, and is sensible and reliable in emergencies, although sometimes inclined to take on too much.

A firm or unbending set of knuckles not only suggests caution, but the type who can be a little too rigid in attitude, someone responsible, but who does not welcome change. While stubborn, even slightly selfish, they are trustworthy and can keep a secret.

Thick and Thin

Thick fingers, especially at the base phalange, betray a love of all the good things of life, selfish people who are ruled by their appetites. If the phalange is overdeveloped, habits can be gross.

When the basal phalange of the fingers is slim, tastes are more refined: the owners like the good things, but in moderation. They prefer quality to quantity, and it shows.

When held naturally, gaps may be seen between the fingers at the basal phalanges. This is a fairly reliable indication that dietary control is poor. These people may not care a lot about what they eat or, for that matter, when. If the fingers are all thin, then, of course, there will be gaps to be seen. Here, attention to diet and associated matters take on a different perspective, for overconcern with food intake can rule their life.

When there is a gap between the middle phalanges, it shows a lot of thought goes into all new ideas and other information as it comes in. It does not follow that the right responses are made, but shows the owner does stop to think and will not blindly dash off.

It is always best to observe the fingers from the front and back because you need to assess the relationship to each other, their neighbours and other parts of the hand. You must also compare the fingers of both hands to each other.

Sensitivity Pads

Sensitivity pads look like small droplets of flesh that appear on the palmar side of the top phalange of the fingers and thumb. It is rare to see a full set. As a rule, they are seen on just one or two fingers. When present, they indicate a highly developed sense of touch.

They emphasise emotional extremes of temperament according to the qualities of the fingers upon which they are found. When a full set is seen, expect to find an instinctive and highly-developed sense of refinement in all the owner does or thinks. He or she may not necessarily have artistic ability, but will be artistically sensitive and have a love of good music or places where works of art are displayed.

These pads are associated with special gifts, the nature of which varies according to the finger on which they are found. When the centre of the pad is placed high on the phalange, the gift will be associated with the subject's intellectual powers. Thinking is aesthetic and defined: the owner is astute and very careful to say or do the right thing at the right time. Taste in dress and appearance will always show.

If the droplet seems to be low set, any refinement will show in the owner's practical abilities – a gift for cooking or setting a table, arranging flowers, and so on.

When the pad is centrally placed, special gifts are demonstrated in an ability to design, create and carry through an exercise to its natural conclusion, like dress-making, for example.

13
The Thumb

The thumb is often called "the signature of the hand", for it is the principal key to character and personality assessment. The thumb is a human development. It opposes the fingers and, by doing so, places man in a unique position. Without it, there is not much we can achieve. But with it, we manipulate and hold or employ the thumb in so many different ways every time we use our hands.

In palmistry, it shows how we control ourselves in our behaviour patterns, or otherwise. It also reveals our vitality, willpower, reason and logic. It indicates whether we have the ability to be a leader or be content to follow.

The thumb must always be assessed in relation to the rest of the hand on which it is found and to its partner on the other hand. Quite often, a weak right hand thumb is offset by the stronger-looking left hand partner, or vice versa. If there is a well-developed, robust-looking thumb on the right hand partnered by a weaker left hand version, it indicates a most positive character. The owner will have worked very hard to have achieved his aims, taking every opportunity to make the most of everything that has come his way.

If a strong left hand thumb is partnered by a weak-looking right hand version, it suggest problems in persuading others, or knowing how to time events to best advantage. Initiating action is rarely well-planned and the subject loses heart easily.

Thus, when there are two strong thumbs it shows a difficult and stubborn nature, one not easily swayed, but who appreciates the direct approach. Two weak thumbs indicate vacillation, someone who bends with the wind no matter how changeable it might be.

The thumb also represents reserves of physical energy, and our power of assertion and willpower. Its shape, position and relative size indicate not only how much of these forces are available, but also how well we have learned to use them. A long, powerful thumb suggests we have plenty of these forces and employ them to the best of our ability. A small but weak-looking thumb indicates the reverse.

There are only two main phalanges to the thumb because the ball of the thumb is more properly called the mount of Venus. We will deal with that a little later.

The first two phalanges should, wherever possible, be equally matched. The nail phalange informs of the willpower available while the lower one shows how we reason and decide how best to use it.

If the lower phalange is larger or longer than the nail section, it indicates that reason tends to prevail more than action. Diplomacy and reason are employed when needed. A nail phalange larger than the other shows the owner acts first and asks questions later, a case of "I want – and I shall have".

But irrespective of which is the larger, if the lower phalange has a definite waisted look to it, this is lessened somewhat, and the owner will always exhibit some diplomacy before taking action.

The length of the thumb ought to be approximately equal to that of the little finger or, when held close to the hand, should reach at least halfway up the third phalange of the first finger.

A flexible or supple tip shows an impulsive nature, someone who is all things to all men. A stiff tip to the thumb suggests a strict disciplinarian, folk not always able to compromise and perhaps a little difficult to understand. They are such hard people to get along with: just living with them needs a lot of patience and understanding!

When the tip bends outward, the nature is open and generous, the mind receptive. If the tip turns inward, the owner will seem rather petty, mean and selfish.

A square tip shows a realist and a hard taskmaster, one who tends to lead by example. They would be unlikely to ask anyone who works for them to do anything they themselves cannot do. There is always a strong sense of justice and fair play.

A spatulate tip on the thumb always refers to the craftsman, those who are practical and know how to get things done. When there is a conic tip, they tend to respond easily (perhaps too much so) to all kinds of external stimuli – colour, shape and sound.

A pointed thumb tip indicates an idealist, one who appears to be submissive. While they may seem weak, these individuals make up for it with the knack of being able to spot the weakness of others and seize the advantage.

The spoke-shave thumb tip tapers toward the top and is best seen from the side. People with this formation have a special ability to get others to undertake things they might not ordinarily do. When any motive is questioned later, they shrug their shoulders and smile enigmatically.

A bulbous tip here shows a very basic and physical approach to life. There are very strong appetites, and what these people want, they have. Opposition is futile and, in some cases, quite dangerous.

They have a dreadful temper and are capable of blind fury. But when they do explode, the whole thing is likely to be over almost as soon as it starts. Take care in your dealings with these folk, for they are utterly ruthless in the pursuance of an aim.

In a relaxed position, the thumb should form an angle of at least 45° to 90° to the index finger. Less than this is narrow and can imply small-mindedness, prejudice, poor perception, selfishness and a limited response.

When the angle is greater than 90° the subject is more resolute and firm, blessed with all the natural and instinctive qualities of leadership.

Position

This is important. The lower the set of the thumb on the side of the hand, the more inspirational the character. If combined with a wider than usual angle, it indicates the adventurous type with a strong sense of self-preservation. Should this angle be narrow, the subject will use every trick in the book to keep that sense active.

A high-set thumb indicates a clearly defined sense of creativity with a good, instinctive flair. The high-set thumb combined with a narrow angle shows the owner knows how to use the tricks of his trade to protect himself at all times. Such individuals tend to break or re-write the rules to suit themselves at the time.

Observe the alignment of the thumb with the fingers because when held naturally, the thumb either aligns or opposes them. Should it appear to be in line with the fingers, the nature is more spontaneous and enthusiastic.

Those with this configuration prefer to pursue pleasure more than their obligations. If the thumb is also high set, they are likely to drop everything at the slightest opportunity to go off and enjoy some new venture.

When the thumb opposes the fingers or stands at right angles to them, there is great personal self-control, possibly too strong. It can be rather difficult to get to know people with this kind of finger/thumb setting, for they always maintain a continuous and conscious self-control in all aspects of their life.

No matter how open they may appear, few realise just how much the opposite is true. These folk have very few friends. Those who do get close must never break their trust. If they do, the relationship can never be on the same footing again.

The base phalange, the mount of Venus, should be firm and springy to the touch, resilient, full and well-developed. This represents the seat of physical emotion and energy. It therefore follows that the more developed this is, the greater the energy available to meet the challenges of life.

When the base phalange greatly outweighs the other two, the subject's physical appetites are likely to interfere with normal life. They know how to enjoy the good life and very little gets in their way when they are in full swing.

If the mount seems flat and thin, the opposite of this will be true – the nature seems flat and lifeless, and appears cold, with little regard for the feelings of others. A selfish streak prevails. There is little or no appreciation of art. If it is not practical, these people have no use for it.

14

The Mounts of the Hand

The mounts are the developed fleshy pads just below each of the four fingers and at the base of the hand just above the wrist. One of these pads is really the third phalange of the thumb and better known as the mount of Venus.

A pronounced bulge or bowing effect at the outer edge of the palm is called the creative curve and is also dealt with as a mount.

It would be extremely rare to find the pure mount type. From time to time people may be seen with rather well-developed pads while others are quite flat.

The creative curve

A noticeable bulge may be observed at the percussion side of the hand. It can stretch from the top to the bottom of the hand. It may be more developed at the top of the palm or more pronounced at the base of the hand. At other times, the central point of the curve sits squarely in the middle of the outer edge.

The full curve indicates good, original creative energies, one able to conceive, design and complete an artistic project or scheme with ease. When the curve is more developed toward the top of the palm, the creativity is more in the mind, someone able to come up with ideas when asked.

Should the curve be more pronounced in the middle of the palm, it indicates someone who is able to design, to take the theory and apply the ideas in a practical manner. If the curve is more to the base of the outer edge of the hand, the subject is better able physically to make the idea(s) come alive.

A completely straight edge to the outside of the palm shows an inability to adapt to new ideas or plans. There is little or no creative ability present.

The 'mouse' or health mount

When the hand is clenched into a fist with the thumb held at the side of the first finger, a small bulge is created at the back of the hand between the thumb and the first finger.

If this is firm to the touch on both hands, it shows the owner currently enjoys good health. Mostly, this person avoids catching all the little bugs and viruses that go the rounds at some time or another.

Should this mount feel soft to the touch on the right hand but still reasonably firm on the left, the subject will be slightly under par. This is likely to be anything from simple tiredness or the occasional long, hard day that we all suffer from time to time. After a good meal and adequate rest we get back to normal – and the mount firms up again.

If the mount feels soft to the touch on the left hand compared with a firm version on the right, it shows the constitution is weakened with temporary illness, like a cold or flu, perhaps. The owner may also be emotionally or intellectually down.

When the mounts on both hands are soft to the touch, the nature is rather negative. The owner doesn't get much out of life, but may not put much in either. There is a lack of enthusiasm: the personality seems lack-lustre.

The mount of Jupiter
If reasonably developed with a centrally placed apex in the skin pattern, the owner is ambitious, honourable, connected socially and fond of good living.

When overdeveloped, the person will seem arrogant and selfish, and expect everyone to do his bidding. Everything must go his way or he will be quite rude and direct. Jewellery and possessions are ostentatious. If in a position of responsibility or leadership, these people have favourites and may be tyrannical at times.

A poorly-developed mount, flat or lifeless looking, indicates a lazy nature. This type lacks a common decency in their dealings with others, and is inclined to take the easy way every time.

The mount of Saturn
A well-developed mount here suggests a rather fatalistic nature. The owners are careful with possessions and money, prudent and more sensitive than average. They prefer to operate away from the glare of the limelight, and are usually found working in the background. Research work also attracts.

If the mount is overdeveloped, a solitary nature is likely. These characters shun an active social life, unless it is necessary to be seen in public. Inwardly, they are inclined toward a love of mystery, secret or occult matters.

When the mount is hardly present at all, they may be a "doubting Thomas", prone to spreading doom and gloom wherever they go. It is almost as if these individuals do not have feelings. Such folk are far from sparkling personalities.

The mount of Apollo

A well-developed mount of Apollo is a strong indication of artistic inclinations. The arts are fanatically pursued. If money and position are available, these people are likely to be a benefactor in some way, similar to a theatrical "angel" perhaps. Once these folk put their minds to something, they are capable of great things.

An overdeveloped mount shows a misplaced sense of self-importance and an assumed greatness and extravagance. The owner can be very quick-tempered, especially if a slight should occur, even if it were unintentional.

A poorly-developed Apollo mount is a clear sign of materialism and a selfish nature. There is very little artistic appreciation, but what there is might well be vulgar.

The mount of Mercury

When this mount is well-developed or centrally placed – a rarity because it tends to share this area with the Apollo mount – there is a flair for commercial matters and/or dealing with money.

Communication of any kind is good. Anything to do with electronic systems like computers, fax machines, telephones, scanners, etc., is second nature. Usually very perceptive, they instinctively know how to deal with people.

An overdeveloped mount suggests an element of deception in their make-up: they are not as honest with themselves or others as they could or should be. Occasionally, if the little finger is crooked, these folk are not always honest – full stop!

This is also a sign of belief in, or a fear of, superstition. If the Mercury mount is flat, there is a poor grasp of business affairs, communication abilities are low, self-motivation weak and any attempt at enterprise way below the average.

The mount of Venus

In reality, this is the lower phalange of the thumb. If it is well-developed, there will be a strong, healthy libido with a good, instinctive sense of affection and a love of family life and home matters generally.

When overdeveloped, the owner will be shameless, over-sexed and not mindful of his or her manners when in company. Social graces are at a very low level.

A flat and lifeless look to the mount shows a poor appreciation of art in any form. Such folk are not really good when it comes to socialising. They might be better off if they lived on their own. It is difficult for them to share things, for they can be so selfish.

There are two clearly defined angles of time to be found at the side of the base of the thumb. Dependent on development, they will show the level of the owner's sense of time, or lack of it. The upper angle suggests a sense of rhythm whilst the lower angle has more to do with a sense of harmony. Either way, music usually plays a fair part in this person's life, perhaps as a performer or alternatively simply because they like it.

The mount of the Moon

Also called the Luna mount, if high and fleshy it shows a rich and highly-developed imagination and restlessness. Some introspection is possible. An excessively developed mount means a changeable nature. It is difficult to get started on anything, but very easy to stop at the slightest whim.

There is a lack of staying power. Willpower is poor and they are easily side-tracked. There is a lack of "get-up-and-go".

A flat or low Luna mount suggests a cold fish, and poor imaginative powers, with little or no sensitivity to the wants and needs of others. The easy way is the best as far as they are concerned. Few original ideas come readily, but plagiarism comes easily.

The zone of Mars

This is the centre of the palm that lies below the digital mounts at the top of the mounts of Luna and Venus, a combination of the old-style mounts of Mars, Positive and Negative, and the Plain of Mars.

A well-developed area here shows the owner has very good powers of resistance, with plenty of energy to pursue favourite indoor or outdoor activities. There is always a sense of fair play.

73

It can be difficult to keep up with such folk. They seem to have far-reaching reserves of physical and emotional energy to help them keep going as they pursue these objectives.

An over-developed zone of Mars is not so good, for there may be an excess of misplaced zeal, a rebel streak perhaps, or just a plain and simple defiance at the slightest remark. They can be innately cruel, with a tendency to exaggerate and be awkward.

If this zone is under-developed, there is a lack of moral fibre and courage. These people may be unable to fight for what they feel is rightfully theirs. They back away from confrontation and may seem childish, with a kind of "front" that puts others off.

The mount of Neptune

With normal development here, the personality will reflect good perceptive abilities. He instinctively deals with people at all levels in almost any circumstance. Such an individual understands what makes people "tick" and knows how to deal with them.

An overdeveloped mount suggests delusions of adequacy far beyond their real abilities, for they talk themselves into and out of situations they cannot possibly handle properly. These types give the impression of having more ability than they actually possess. They can bluff so well!

An under-developed mount of Neptune shows the owner has little sensitivity for anything mystical. He scorns superstition and in some cases may even refute the comfort of a religious belief.

The mount of Pluto

This is a rather modern innovation that treats the bottom third of the Luna mount as a separate mount in its own right. When it is normal, full and well-developed, it suggests a practical and theoretical interest in occult or secret doctrines. It is also a sign of patriotism, especially if very full.

There may be a racist attitude in the sense that the owner would prefer *all* non-nationals to be shipped out of the country. There is nothing personal in this, just a plain and simple dislike of foreigners. They can visit, but they may not stay.

When flat or under-developed, the owner is likely to oppose or scoff at subjects like astrology, palmistry or similar matters.

Part Two
CHIROMANCY

15

The Lines on the Hand

This brief introduction to the lines on the hand is to show how it is possible to elaborate on assessments made from the shape and general formation of the hand.

The principal lines – head, heart and life – begin to form early in pregnancy. By about twenty weeks, most babies will begin to have some semblance of markings in their palms.

The lines represent a direct relationship with our genetic inheritance. We have some, if not all, of the lines etched in the palm of our hands. The real difference between someone's hands will be reflected by the way each person's character and personality develops.

Any pronounced development of a particular line or lines will go to show which area of our character has more strength or has taken on a greater significance. For example, a conic hand, which indicates emotional sensitivity, usually has a fine tracery of many lines. But on a square hand, which refers to a much more placid and practical approach to life, one would expect to see only a few lines.

Thus, a conic hand with a bare few lines is a sure indication that the owners obviously have plenty of self-assurance and self-reliance. They would possess a good constitution and a fair balance between their nervous and physical energies. However, a square hand with many lines suggests a most sensitive and impressionable nature, perhaps artistically inclined, but with a possible excess of nervous and physical energy.

Equally, it would be very unusual to find a fine tracery of lines on an elementary hand because we associate this with very basic actions and philosophies. Mostly, the best one can find on such a hand is head, heart and line of life, together with a few influence lines and even fewer minor lines.

On a psychic hand, because the nature is so full of vivid imagery and sensitivity, one would expect to find it covered with lines going hither and thither in all directions.

THE LINES ON THE HAND

A hand print showing the principal lines of the hand.

AA   Line of Life
BB   Line of Head
CC   Line of Heart
DD   Line of Fate
E   Sun Line
F   Mercury Line

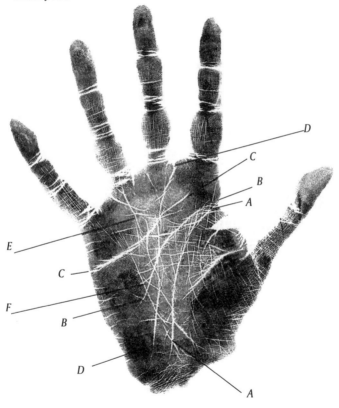

A spatulate hand tends to have a fair share of lines to indicate in which direction the owner's inclinations may lie, mentally or physically. The more lines there are on a hand, the more mental activity there will be. Just a few lines show a physically active personality.

Meanwhile, the philosophic hand almost always has rather fine lines, with a few quite deeply marked, showing a greater capacity for thought. Thus, on this hand, the lines appear in a directed rather than a haphazard fashion across the palm.

Observe these simple rules as you proceed with your analysis and you will find it much easier to delineate character and personality.

Left hand/right hand

It is generally accepted in palmistry that the left hand denotes inherited and natural inclinations. The development, or lack of it, as well as the shape and the lines on this hand will show what talents and desires are available.

The right hand indicates how these gifts have been developed by the owner, if at all. Other talents may lie dormant until much later in life. In cases where both hands have a similar appearance, it is safe to assume that the subjects have made or desired little change. These folk are prone to lead a quiet and peaceful life.

The more dissimilar a pair of hands, the more change the owner has imposed. Once it is established there are significant differences between them, you must study each hand closely for the cause.

Vastly differing head lines may also be accompanied by basic hand shape differences, but this is not always or necessarily the case. However, if this is seen, it is a clear indication that the owner has had to face many obstacles to achieve his or her aims.

Assessing the differences and gauging the extent of the problems which the subject has had to overcome is often difficult at first, but becomes easier with time.

If the lines of life are considerably different, the problems are probably of a domestic or family origin. You may be able to trace the beginning of these in early childhood. Problems with either or both parents, brothers or sisters, or the educational regime are the probable causes. Alternatively, this can indicate health problems.

In cases where the two heart lines show noticeable differences, the root cause is almost certainly to be an emotional one. It should not take long to assess the extent of the power of the subject's emotional considerations in regard to his or her decision-making. Someone else – or a string of other people – may have consistently ridden roughshod over the subject and made their life thoroughly miserable. It could be the reverse: they might have ridden over others to ensure they got their own way!

The clearer the lines the better. Think of them as power cables because wherever there is an obstruction the current is impeded. When a line divides and reconnects later, the period of the island it creates indicates the time of the weakening of its power.

Cross-bars, cuts, dots, tassels and fraying all indicate a loss of the full potential of the line. A clean break is a warning. If seen on both hands, it indicates serious trouble ahead. Should the line continue after any break, the problem will have left its mark on the subject and shall do so for some time after the event.

Other markings in the hand will confirm or ease the situation and should be read in conjunction with the broken line. Bear in mind that the colour of a line has an effect on its relative strengths and weaknesses as well.

Reddish lines strongly etched into the palm suggest a positive personality, firm and resolute with a dislike of opposition. This character is one who knows how to get his own way. Pale lines suggest a lack of vitality along with a vapid or negative nature, and are usually found on a soft or finely textured skin.

The lines on the hands can – and do – change with time. As we grow older and experience life, they record our triumphs and disasters and remain in our memory to remind us of certain pitfalls or signposts to better things.

It is always practical and wise, therefore, to keep a permanent record of these changes by making prints of the hands at regular intervals. There are many ways of taking and keeping hand-prints. These are dealt with elsewhere.

Occasionally, you may see hands with one or more of the principal lines missing or so faint as to be practically non-existent. In that event, the line or lines thus affected will become a focal point in the personality and nature of the subject.

An absent or poorly formed line of life indicates a lack of zeal, or poor or recurring health problems, like a permanent disability, for example.

An absent or poorly formed line of head shows an an inability to concentrate for long periods of time while a heart line affected in a similar fashion refers to a poor emotional life, or possibly a weakened vascular system.

Lines should be carefully examined, preferably under a powerful magnifying glass. Of course, whenever possible try to take hand prints. They are so useful for cross-reference purposes when studying a particular problem.

Full or empty hands

When you look at a hand, you should be able to see immediately if it is a "full" or "empty" hand. A full hand looks just that – full of all kinds of lines that crisscross all over the palm. This is a sign of a worrier. The mind is rarely still: it is difficult for the owner to switch off when the time comes.

The imagination is always active and vivid, the nature highly emotional and sensitive to a fault. Often, such people lack confidence. There is an in-built distrust of those around them. These characters are perceptive and understanding. While quite clever, they lack the initiative to get them going – but then such individuals know how to bluff.

The "empty" hand barely has the three principal lines, perhaps with a few small influence lines or marks dotted here and there. These people do not seem to feel things as deeply as those with full hands. Not much excites them: there is little open emotional display. They can be quite tenacious. Once starting something, they finish it!

These people are best suited to disciplined work like the police or the armed services, for they are conventional and able to give and take orders with equal facility. For the most part, they are straightforward, orderly, punctual and enjoy a quiet life. Some are creative and practical, but not always appreciated or noticed because they are so quiet and so unassuming.

16
The Head Line

There are three principal lines on the hand – the head, heart and life. Of these, I have always considered the line of head to be the most important. The accepted measure of intelligence in the hand, it shows the owner's ability to think and reason things through. The level of perception, depth of imagination and mental flexibility are to be found here.

We all think in different ways and, as a result, adopt differing approaches to life's problems. Because of this, the line of head can begin at any one of many different points in the hand and set its own path across the palm to end almost anywhere.

The right hand line will show the development of the owner's mind in the conscious and active direction that has been adapted from the latent or inherited gifts as indicated by the unconscious, or passive, left hand.

The right hand also reveals how the subject has adopted these talents, and how education and experience have had their respective effects on the personality. The left hand head line shows to what extent the subject will exercise his intellect before it becomes over-stretched or tired, unable to cope.

Differences between these two lines, therefore, refer to changes in life. The more they are different, the greater the number of changes the owner has had to make.

If the weaker-looking line of the two is on the left hand, then the owner has used a lot of willpower in efforts to break away from restrictive elements in the earlier part of life. How this has been achieved will be shown in other parts of the hand. When the weaker-looking line is on the right, the owner is likely to have a less positive personality.

The ideal head line starts cleanly and clearly just touching – or very near – the line of life, sweeps out into the palmar plain in a smooth but slightly bowing effect, and ends at a point below the middle of the fourth finger. It should be clear of all dots, cross bars, spots and other marks of influence, except for the vertical lines one expects to find in the hand as a matter of course. This subject will have good perceptive abilities and values, be sensible and intelligent, and possess a reasonable approach to all aspects of life.

The head line may be short and finish somewhere under the middle finger, or might stretch right across the palm to end on the lower edge of the Luna mount. On some hands, there may be two, three or no line of head at all. It could start as suggested and split into a huge island across the palm to reunite near its end.

A short head line which ends under the middle finger is not seen very often on a conic hand. It is associated more with the square or useful hand. When seen, the owner will approach problems sensibly and practically. He or she will also have a good memory and able to concentrate for long spells at a time.

The longer, sloping line that bows slightly is far more likely to be seen on the conic or round hand. While the owner finds it hard to concentrate, he does enjoy a variety of interests, but rarely stays with one for very long. Although there is an inability to concentrate, there is often a good investigative mind.

The short head line suggests specialist interests while a long line implies a more diverse approach. With the longer line, there is a more flexible nature. Such people are co-operative and easy to get along with, and are usually prepared to compromise.

Compare a six-inch ruler with a twelve- and eighteen-inch version. The small one hardly bends at all, but the other two bend more readily, the longer one more so as a matter of course. Like the short ruler, the short head line tends to be inflexible, yields less in negotiation and does not compromise very easily at all. These types are logical: some may be cold by nature.

Either way, whether it is a short or a long line, if it is also wavy it denotes a sense of insecurity. The subject is conscious of this all the time and unable to rid himself of such thoughts. Should the line become straight after a wavy period, he becomes more in control of his life. This individual will also be known for a resentful attitude, and spends a lot of time seemingly unsatisfied, carping, criticising and complaining about something or someone.

Lines that branch or fork show a diversification of the principal interests in life: the wider the fork, the more wide-ranging the interests become. If the line separates into several small lines, there will be many interests to occupy the mind. However, the owner seems unable to concentrate adequately for very long on any of them. If the line should fray, a dissipation of intellectual energies occurs, time and effort are wasted, and new projects come to nothing if, indeed, they ever get off the ground in the first place.

When the head line starts inside the line of life, the nature will be subjective rather than objective. This person does not like to step out of line or take chances, and is a follower, not a leader.

However, there is often an innate sense of courage. Should this line be on the left hand only, there will be a presence of mind with a good sense of determination whereby this person can – and does – take charge in an emergency. This character stands out and is remembered when any catastrophe strikes. But when it is all over, he retreats back into his unassuming ways once again.

If found on the right hand only, this trait will be more positive ... and heaven help anyone who tries to bully him! Not only will the bully be put in his place, but it will done in a such a way that no one is allowed to forget it.

A head line that begins tied to the life line for some way is a sure indication of caution, dependence, indecision and worry. The owner is subjectively inclined, and emotionally inhibited, with a way of bottling things up so that others may not notice. In business, very little is left to chance. Slowly but surely, such characters succeed in a venture where others might easily fail.

A head line that starts a small distance away from the life line shows a greater degree of independence, with more confidence and self-sufficiency. Here is someone who is well able to think for himself with any emotional considerations put to one side.

When the gap is wide, a rash or over-confident nature prevails, for he or she is impulsive and dislikes restriction. Considered unreliable because they are inclined to take short cuts or bend the rules to suit themselves, they can be quite ruthless and very calculating. They allow nothing to get in the way of their aims. The wider the gap, the more this will be so.

Sometimes, the head and life line are tied together at the start, with a chaining affect. This implies emotional dependence: few get to know the real inner character. Often, these types are unable to express their emotions properly. This may be due to an incident that could have happened within the family when still quite young.

A head line that starts on the mount of Jupiter indicates pride, drive and some aggression. The owner can think for himself, but does not always take into account the effect this may have on others.

When the head line starts high and remains high on the palm close to the heart line, it shows the owner is always aware of the need for security in every sense of the word. This is the sort who buys two of everything in case the first one should fail.

A low-starting head line from just inside or barely touching the life line that moves over the palm in an upward movement towards the little finger indicates an avaricious nature. Here, the owner is acquisitive, materialistic and very possessive. When money comes in, this character has a gift making even more – and keeping it.

Because a line can vary so much, even on the same hand, it may be difficult to analyse. If you remember the analogy of a line as a power cable, it is much easier to understand that any obstruction or weakening of appearance detracts from its full meaning.

A weak, fluffy and pale line shows an inability to concentrate. This owner can have trouble switching off at night. Sleeping habits are poor. The mind is rarely still, even when he or she is supposed to be at ease and relaxed. Non-essential matters or trivia can take up much of their time.

Where other lines cross the head line, like the fate line, check the conjunction carefully. If the fate line looks dissimilar to the head line at this point, career trouble – or the career itself – could be a problem.

A close examination may reveal small influence lines running back and forth between them. If these little lines stem from the life line side of the fate line, family and friends may be the source of any problems. If these marks occur on both sides of the fate line, the pressure will be strong. When the lines originate from the other side of the fate line, any outside influences will be from business or career associates.

Should the fate line stop at the head line, a wrong decision was made with serious consequences, unless the head line looks much clearer after this conjunction. If this is the case, the worries should be over and the owner able to get on with his life. This is seen more on a conic hand than anywhere else and suggests the owner was pressured into a position he did not really want in the first place, but was unable to resist those who influenced him. Alternatively, it might belong to someone who sought an important position through bluff and subsequently paid the penalty, for these folk cannot hold down top jobs for very long.

A break in the head line is a sign of a head injury and, if on both hands, can indicate an accident, breakdown or illness. If the break is surrounded by a square, the problem is likely to be less severe because a square acts as a protecting influence. Nevertheless, the subject can never forget the incident no matter what the outcome.

Any island formation on the head line suggests a weakening of the power of the line which would be restored once the island ends. Occasionally, a head line will start normally, then split into a large island before re-forming again just before it ends. This is often seen on the hands of those who have had to live a lie for most of their lives, either from choice or because they were forced to. This will have a far-reaching and serious implication, and one needs to ascertain its cause.

A head line that forks at the end suggests two opposing forces at work. The mind is lively, active and balanced. It is ideal for an investigator or a researcher, especially if the line is straight or short. On the longer or sloping line, it shows someone able to follow two different careers at the same time. Sometimes called "the writer's fork", it is not limited just to literary ability.

Tradition says that if one of the forks touches the outer edge of the palm, the owner will be recognised for his talents abroad, for good or ill. The wider the fork, the stronger the possibility the career will not reflect the subject's real aim in life.

When the head line sweeps straight across the palm as if cutting it in two, it shows a character whose mental powers control all responses, even if the line slopes a little. When this marking is seen in both hands, take care: you will be dealing with someone whose mental strength can – and will – override all emotional considerations if it is deemed necessary, irrespective of any other contradictory line formation. This is called the Sydney line.

A head line that dips and sweeps down the palm to the base of the Luna mount always indicates a more than fertile imagination: the deeper the sweep, the more active the mind. Some emotional and mental imbalance will be present. Staying with reality may not always be easy.

Occasionally, a head line will pass straight over the palm to end along the top of the Luna mount, roughly under the Apollo finger. This, in turn, may be met by a sloping fate line that starts from the outer edge of the lower part of the Luna mount.

This is a suggestion of indecision. The subject can make as many statements or take as many decisions as he likes, but after the event, an element of doubt creeps into his thinking, and the more he wonders if he did or said the right thing.

As a line ends, it may simply fade, tasselate or fray. This is in keeping with the natural weakening of the mental powers as age takes its toll, not senility as such, but a reluctance to absorb information.

A line with a chained formation shows poor concentration. If this is along all of the line, the owner should never try to hold down a position of authority. A chaining effect for a short distance is a reflection of a temporary loss of mental strength, which returns as the head line resumes its natural formation and course.

Influence lines that rise from the line always show an effort is made to improve life-style. Lines that fall away imply a loss of opportunity.

There are many other variations on a theme. Where a configuration occurs that has not been dealt with here, take time to assess the problem and apply the nearest in meaning that you find.

In essence, always remember that the more positive the line, the more positive the nature. The poorer the quality of the line, the less mental ability is available to the subject.

17
The Heart Line

The heart line is associated with all emotional matters in the personality and character, some health factors and the vascular system generally.

It may start from anywhere on the mount of Jupiter, between the first and second fingers, on the extreme edge of the hand between the thumb and first finger, or could have a forked beginning. In a few cases, it may rise on the mount of Saturn.

The line might be long, short, thick or thin, and can appear to be chained or full of little islands. It should be clear of all the little influence lines save for those that are expected to cross it in the normal manner. It often has tiny influence lines that may rise or fall from it all along its course.

The emotional nature
When the heart line begins from the Jupiter mount and follows a gentle, even curve all the way to the percussion with few or no interference marks, it shows that the subject's basic emotional nature is well-balanced.

There will be some idealism, but this all depends on the course of the line. The further it reaches downward into the palm, the more physically expressive the nature. Conversely, the higher it remains on the palm under the fingers, the greater the mental approach.

A deeply etched line that looks darker in colour when compared to the other two major lines almost always implies problems of a vascular nature. The nails will confirm this, for it means an erratic approach to relationships. It may also suggest that the subject can suffer from hypertension

When both the heart and head lines are set low on the palm but a fairly wide gap remains, the owner will be ruled more by his head than his heart. Extremes of temperament are likely, especially if all is not well. This type does not always react as other people might expect.

Should the heart line be set high on the palm and hardly curves at all, the nature is inclined to be rather hard and cold. This is especially so if the head line is also set high. When the two lines stay close together, the nature is coldly dispassionate and possessive. The lower the start of the heart line, the greater this will be in evidence. The higher on the palm the line starts, the more the nature is idealistic.

Often, the heart line forks at its commencement. One line starts on the mount of Jupiter while the other reaches out toward the radial side of the hand between the thumb and the first finger, suggesting emotional adaptability. When one line comes from the mount of Saturn and the other from the Jupiter mount – a frequent occurrence – it all depends which is the heavier or more stronger-looking branch.

If the fork from Jupiter is the stronger, there will be an honest and upright approach to all forms of relationships. When the Saturn fork is the stronger line, the owner is more practical and straightforward in dealings with people. The fork itself indicates someone who favours a career in social work, a teacher, nurse or an occupation where the subject cares for people, but is rather reluctant, unwilling or unable to become closely or emotionally involved.

A deeply etched or curved heart line that begins from the mount of Saturn indicates a strongly sensual nature. But such folk can appear to be quite cold emotionally and are capable of using people for their own ends. They seem unable to recognise or acknowledge the sensitive side of other individuals. This selfishness leads them to cater to their own desires and satisfaction most of the time.

Tradition has it that a three-pronged start to the line is lucky and good fortune will always be with the owner. In many ways this is so, but always look for an influence line that starts from the lowest prong and goes to the head line. If it is there, it shows disappointments in emotional affairs.

When the head, heart and life lines are joined at their beginning, it should be regarded as a warning. At some time in life, the owner will experience a sudden and perhaps quite traumatic shock from which he or she may never fully recover – an event that leaves its mark forever, emotionally, mentally and physically. Sometimes, the lines may be observed to start this configuration, suggesting that in the very near future, such an event will occur.

A short or faintly marked line of heart line shows a cold nature. There could be a short, sharp temper ... and not very well controlled at that! If the line starts on or under the mount of Saturn, the emotions are based on physical attraction throughout life. These people are not easily fooled, can show a surprising level of under-standing and always have their feet firmly on the ground.

Acute possessiveness will be likely when the line starts at the extreme edge of the hand, anywhere between the mounts of Mars and Jupiter. The further it reaches to the other side of the hand, the more the owner remains blind to the imperfection of those he loves. The straighter the line, the more this is emphasised. When this line starts and stays low across the palm, the subject will be very aware of the failings of others.

But if this line stays high on the top of the palm, a cold and calcu-lating nature, hard and with little or no feeling, will be in evidence. The nature is such that all matters are undertaken and completed regardless of any emotional consideration. You cannot appeal to a better nature: these people do not have one, and are difficult to get to know intimately.

Sometimes, small lines may fall away or cross the heart line near its commencement. Either way this indicates a need for constant stimulation, variety and change. This suggests it will be found more on a conic or spatulate hand than anything else, but it can occur with the other shapes as well.

These people have a wide variety of acquaintances and contacts, and a superficial knowledge of many subjects because if a person or topic catches their fancy, they will pursue either until they tire. Thus, they may seem to be interesting for a while, but there is no depth of character at all.

The straighter the line, the more assertive and firm the general attitude. The emotional approach is down-to-earth and practical: the owner takes life as it comes.

The square hand usually has the straighter line, suggesting more resolution, someone not easily swayed by anything, save perhaps common sense. Feelings are just as deeply felt, but logic tends to rule most of the time. This type is not easily fooled. A curved line suggests a greater sense of imagination. The owner is more receptive, accessible and flexible in dealings with others.

As a rule, the conic hand tends to have the curved head line. This suggests a demonstrative, emotional nature, plenty of imagination, someone free with all those little personal touches and gestures in a close relationship.

A straight line on a conic hand shows an intensity of feeling and emotional expression, especially if the line is deeply marked. A faint line may reveal an inner cold nature, but you only find out about it when it is too late! Possessive and loyal, this usually only continues for as long as the "interest" lasts.

Always compare the right hand heart line with its partner on the left. Look for the more basic or subtle differences as this will tell you which way your subject now leans, emotionally speaking.

If there are no real differences, the owner is content with his emotional relationships and does not actively seek further experiences. He may dream, but that will be as far as it goes.

The health factor
As the heart line also has close links with health matters, its appearance and formation along with other features elsewhere in the hand should be examined to give an assessment of the current and potential well-being.

We look to this line for the condition of the vascular system, hearing, sight, mineral deficiency and possible dental problems.

Primarily, the line ought to be clear of all imperfections. There should be no bars, chaining, dots, islands or other influence lines other than those expected to cross it.

A line that consists of islands, chaining, or a series of tiny broken lines refers to poor health. A left hand line that is much stronger than the one on the right will show that health began to deteriorate at the time indicated. The other way round demonstrates the time when it all started to improve.

It is felt by many medical practitioners that when we are physically unwell, we may also be emotionally disturbed as well, which could explain why the heart line is so important in health matters.

A faint or shallow line implies that mental or emotional problems can undermine physical well-being. A dark and deeply etched line suggests that physical problems could be a cause of poor health.

If the palm is covered in a fine tracery of many minor lines it indicates that the subject suffers from nervous energy. These people burn up energy very fast indeed.

An island in the line more or less under the middle finger is an indication of trouble with hearing in some way. If found in both hands this is emphasised. Check the the tip of the little finger for flexibility: a stiff and unyielding tip will confirm possible hearing problems, while the more flexible the tip, the better the hearing. An island under the third finger suggests eye or sight problems.

Traditionally, a circle on the thumb side of the line of life is an indication of sight defects: a half circle suggests one eye only will be affected.

A little further along the line of heart, between the third and fourth fingers, there may be a series of four or five lightly marked small vertical lines just above the line. These nearly always suggest dental problems, usually the gums. Occasionally, these little marks could be confused with the Medical Stigmata, but strictly speaking these are situated nearer the little finger.

The Medical Stigmata stimulates an interest in – or an aptitude for – healing. The subject will be inclined to lean toward a medically-orientated environment or even veterinary work. However, if these little marks refer to neither dental problems nor medical matters, they may well reflect a slight case of hypochondria.

Anxiety, excess weight or faulty blood pressure are shown by a small island in the heart line directly under the little finger. If the heart line is also chained, then a weakness in the vascular system is likely, perhaps confirmed elsewhere in the hand.

I must stress that one must never, ever try to diagnose medical matters unless fully trained to do so. It is a very dangerous practice … and can have far-reaching effects on your subject.

18
The Life Line

Of the three main lines of the hand – the head, heart and life – many authorities consider the life line to be the most important. It will normally reveal the subject's basic approach to life whatever the prevailing conditions. Nevertheless, it still has to be read in conjunction with other characteristics in the hand, and with equal consideration.

For example, if this line appears to be the most strongly marked of the three lines, it should be read that physical matters take precedence over everything else. Such a line is largely to be found on the hands of those who thrive best in the great outdoors.

The line of life may start anywhere on the mount of Jupiter, the mount of Mars or be the dividing mark between them. It might begin in the skin pattern at the edge of the palm or a little further into the palm. It could be clear-cut or start in an islanded or chained fashion.

It should sweep out into the palm, encircling the mount of Venus to end near or at the base of the palm, in one of many different ways. Sometimes, it seems to have a tight hold around the ball of the thumb and end under it. It might sweep out toward the Luna mount or stop as the dividing line between it and the mount of Venus. It can even keep going all the way to the lower outside edge of the palm. At the end it might fork – once, twice or many times – or fray, tasselate, or just simply fade away.

This line must always look strong and healthy and have as few interruptions as possible, for this is the gauge of the subject's natural vitality and zest for living, and indicates a robust or weakened constitution.

A myth or tradition has grown up with this particular line. It is widely believed that a short line means a short life, and a long line, a long life. This is quite wrong. People can – and do – exist with only a token or a very short line while others thrive quite well without any life line at all!

When the line begins as a single line in the skin pattern at the edge of the hand, expect to find a fair level of self-reliance in the overall character. When it starts in a chained formation, the subject tends to be rather dependent on others. If it begins as an open-ended island, there will be a some mystery attached to the birth, illegitimacy, or difficulty with the actual physical birth.

Where the life line seems tied to the head line for a short while, the owner will display caution in all he does. Self-doubt is present, along with a lot of inner sensitivity as well. These folk rarely achieve much success even in their most favoured chosen ambitions.

This can also be taken as a mark of nationalism, for there will be a love of tradition, the right way of doing things, following conventions and resenting those who do not.

As the lines of head and life part, a number of small hair-like influence lines or chains may be seen between them. The more there are, the less self-confident the subject. These people will look to others for leadership because decisiveness is just not one of their strengths.

When the line begins high on the Jupiter mount, there will always be an ambitious streak in the overall nature. Self-confidence is strong, and in extreme cases these individuals think they are infallible. As a result, when things do go wrong, they have to find someone else to blame because they are unable to admit to their own faults. A high start increases these tendencies while a lower beginning inclines the personality to be more natural and friendly.

As a rule, the life line tends to start between the two mounts and acts as the dividing line between them. The character might be slightly less self-assured. The lower this line starts – on the mount of Mars, for example – the greater the indication that the subject is a follower and rarely makes a move without being sure of the facts.

Any influence line that touches or passes through the life line shows disturbance in the owner's life at this point. If the influence is from inside the life line, stemming from the mount of Venus, then a family member or close friend will be responsible for the trouble.

Influence lines from the other side of the line of life need to have their source traced to see from where, or from whom, all the trouble originates. If an influence line originates from the Mercury finger or mount, it may have something to do with work. From Jupiter, the source could be with the hopes, wishes, ambitions, and so on.

As we associate the line of life with the subject's natural verve and energy, look to the course it takes once it begins its path down the hand. It should sweep out into the palm and circle the mount of Venus, dividing it from the palmar plain.

If the line seems to restrict the natural expansion of the mount of Venus, the subject's outlook will also be restricted. Any enthusiasm for life, the natural zeal, will seem to be missing. But do check the line on the other hand for comparison.

When the left hand line seems restrictive and the right hand is noticeably different, many attempts to better the life will have been made. There may have been health weaknesses, or parental or scholastic discipline was too harsh. Quite simply, the early environment was most unsuitable and held him or her back.

However, when the life line in the right hand sweeps out into the palmar surface with little or no ties between it and the line of head, the subject will have made sustained and conscious efforts to gain better personal freedom and self-expression.

He or she will have fought off parental oppression, risen above all restrictions, ensured good health and a responsible diet, and learned to live with weaknesses that could not be overcome.

The reverse of this shows that depleted circumstances have taken their toll and the owner has had to do with whatever was available in personal or material terms. Often, the subject is well aware of all these problems.

Any influence lines rising from the line of life signify efforts to solve the problems or, at the very least, improve matters to make life a little more bearable. If these little influence lines are long enough, they may show in which direction the efforts were made.

A line of life that starts on the mount of Mars and restricts the mount of Venus makes the owner sensitive, touchy, and ready to kick in a self-defensive mechanism at the slightest sign of a problem. Sometimes, when this does not work, these types may exhibit sudden fits of almost hysterical temper when things go wrong. This can also occur if backed into a corner as if they are being bullied, especially when the head and life lines are joined at the start.

Thus, when a life line sweeps right out into the palm in a nicely-shaped curve, it is a strong indication of an extrovert nature. In the case of the straighter, tighter line, it is clearly a sign of introversion.

Occasionally, the life line is seen to start in the normal way, but fades out before it reaches very far into the palm. This mark is nearly always seen on the left hand, rarely on the right hand only. As a rule, it is more common to see it on both hands.

When you look a little further into the palm, you will see that the line appears to run parallel to but ends a short distance from another line. It is this secondary line that is the more important, for it is a new or "home-grown" line of life.

It looks as though it starts from the head line and takes a fairly firm path down the palm to end just about anywhere, much the same as a normal life line might do. This configuration always shows a dissatisfaction with the control, or otherwise, parents imposed on the subject.

When it all gets too much, they just pack their belongings, leave home and make their own way in life. It is also possible that the person left home at the expense of inter-family relationships because he or she tired of the discipline imposed in their formative years.

Because freedom means so much and they think they know best, these characters take this action to prove themselves. Later on in life when these folk have their own families, their offspring will be treated far differently from the way they were, but in some cases this can result in a lack of discipline.

Sometimes, one may see a sister line running parallel with a life line. This is the line of Mars. It runs inside the main line on the mount of Venus, in part or in whole with the main line to help strengthen it, whether or not it is needed. In the hand of an athlete, it gives that extra touch to the physical extras a sportsman needs to call on.

Occasionally, a hand may support two life lines that run parallel almost from start to finish. It means that the subject lives two completely different lives. I have only ever seen this once. It was in the right hand only – and the owner confirmed the assessment.

Once past the midway point down the hand, the line may begin to break up in a number of ways. It can even keep going all the way to the lower outside edge of the palm. At the end it might fork, once, twice or many times, or fray, tasselate, or just simply fade away.

When there is little change in its appearance, the owner is well in control of his life. Little affects him and he bends with the wind quite well. When there is a change, the difference may be obvious and warning sounds should be made.

It is not until middle age that business ambitions are achieved. These new levels of work are much harder to maintain than first realised. Look at the line of life at this point and you will see it may have strengthened, but further down the palm, a line can seem to be breaking up, showing signs of stress and strain.

In this case, the subject has taken on more then he can reasonably be expected to manage. This life line is showing an early warning sign indicating this. The owner must take the necessary steps to ease the situation ... or else!

A line that curves in to finish under the ball of the thumb shows the owner does not dislike travel or being away, but prefers to return home, the one place he feels safe and secure.

When the life line sweeps outward and ends on the Luna mount, there is always a great desire for travel and fresh experiences. It is the clearest mark of travel in the hand, emphasised if in both hands.

A forked end to the life line is a sign of restlessness. If a branch should end on the Luna mount, this will be evident from the subject's lifestyle, hobbies and interests. He may have a job that involves constant change, or a hobby with a similar effect.

Any mark, break, chaining, cross bar, dot, discolouration or an island indicates poor health – a blockage of the vital power of the line. If, after the interruption, the line resumes as before, then the owner has overcome the problem.

When the line deteriorates after this mark, so does the health, but this should be confirmed elsewhere in the hand. Any mark that prevents the natural flow of energy in the line will always indicate trouble. A break may mean an accident – a serious warning if found in both hands. Chaining or changes of colour imply psychological trouble.

Cross bars mean set-backs. A circle or semi-circle suggests eye trouble while a dot shows nervous worries. Islands usually mean a weakened constitution while they last. Fraying or fading indicates the loss of vitality before the end of life.

19
The Fate Line

It is said that there are three principal lines in the hand with the rest catalogued as minor lines, but some are considered more important than others.

The fate line deserves better treatment than this and should be regarded as a special, one-off major influence, for it is the only line that is equally important to note when it is in the hand just as much as when it is not.

None of the other lines has this special quality. An absent line of head, heart and life have no special significance. If not on the hand, they cannot be read. None of the minor lines is so special that they are noticed if not in the hand. But the fate line is very special. It is so inextricably involved with everything regarding character, personality and our overall outlook on life.

Strictly speaking, only the line that starts at the wrist and goes direct to the base of the finger of Saturn should be called the line of fate. All other forms or variations are not strictly fate lines. There are a variety of names – the awareness line, destiny, environment, milieu, direction, or duty lines or marks.

It might be argued that while some of these titles are similar in meaning, where and how they actually appear on the hand does make a difference when it comes to interpretation.

It is rare to find a fate line proper in both hands, but when it is there, it shows how well attuned and aware the subject is to his environment. However, its presence is a restricting factor because the line of fate governs the ambitions.

That means whatever aims the owner has are subject to certain limitations brought about by the amount of self-belief in his or her personal make-up. Thus, the degree of faith in one's abilities is determined by the construction and formation of the line of fate.

The presence of a fate line suggests the subject is able to shoulder his responsibilities as any mature person should. He can create a career which, in turn, will help to maintain his position in society.

When there is no line of fate or its variations, there is almost always a lack of direction – the owner is inwardly unsettled or unsure of himself, with little or no pride. Often, even his personal appearance will leave a lot to be desired.

The fate line will be found in the hands of those whose work requires precision. It is the balance of the hand. The path, which is straight up the centre of the palm, runs exactly between the radial, active side of the hand, and the ulna or unconscious side.

When there is no fate line on either hand, the subject should be given a strict upbringing and taught the difference between right and wrong very early in life. If this person is allowed to grow up to take his place in the adult world without any formal training, he is likely to fritter his life away with a series of unproductive, wasteful jobs.

With short fingers and no fate line, he will feel he has to give only lip service to everything – to get along with the minimum of effort or by taking short cuts that often end in disaster. Only if it becomes absolutely necessary will he stir his bones and make a special effort, but even then it will only be to get over the immediate hurdle facing him.

When the palm is short, there is a long finger of Apollo or the medius is short and spatulate with a very flexible tip, he is inclined to be a gambler. This character muddles through everything. He cannot hold down a job for long, and when he does, it has to be a task that requires very little attention to detail.

If the fate line is on the right hand only, the subject is able to appreciate his lot in either direction. He has the initiative to better himself: the type of hand will show just how he could do this. If on the left hand only, it indicates the owner's aspirations and dreams. But unless there are supportive markings elsewhere, little effort is actually put into pursuing them.

The true fate line starts from the wrist, among the rascettes or bracelets, or can begin from inside the life line on the mount of Venus. Strictly speaking, this now becomes the duty line. For as long as it remains inside the life line, the owner may have to follow family wishes or obligations. The son of a solicitor is expected to follow him into the legal profession. A military man will want his offspring to take up a similar career, and so on. The family business will be carried on – it is the tradition!

If this is the case, take time to examine the fate line closely immediately after it leaves the confines of the life line. When it looks stronger, the youngster has followed the family wishes and is now settled, or at the very least making the most of it.

If, after crossing the life line, the fate line weakens or tails off, the family wishes were observed, at least for a while. Then it all got too much for him and he decided to look elsewhere for something more rewarding – in his eyes!

A careful check of the hand might show another fate line starting at about the time the first one ends. It can be quite faint to begin with, showing a tentative or unsure new beginning. A strong new line is a sign of plenty of confidence in the new venture.

A fate line that crosses the life line then stays close to it for a while shows the subject is content to follow family requirements and make the best of it. A fate line that begins from the line of life itself shows a certain amount of restriction in the early or formative years, but with family support the youngster actively pursues his ambitions. A line like this means the owner has to work hard to achieve his aims. A firm hand helps him to sustain his efforts while a soft hand makes it more difficult.

The higher a fate line starts inside or from the life line, the later the character begins to develop enough determination to go after a chosen aim, to achieve what he wants from life.

The fate line may begin from anywhere on the mount of the Moon. A long, clear line to the base of the middle finger indicates an independent and very determined nature indeed, for this line is a sign that the owner will brook little or no opposition from anyone or anything.

It is likely the chosen career depends on the acceptance of the outside world by working in some way in the public eye, or in an occupation that requires public approbation for success. This could be in local or national politics, or similar, like the Civil Service. It may also be an acting career – stage, screen or TV. An occupation like this needs a lot of faith in oneself. In this case, there is little risk of family interference, not that it matters as the subject would not stand for it, anyway.

There may be another line that appears to start between the line of life and the main fate line, but which stops before it reaches the head line. This milieu line, as it is more correctly known, tends to create problems for as long as it runs.

When present, it stops the subject from achieving his aims. This may be due largely to ill-health or financial restrictions. When the line stops, so do the problems and the owner is free to follow his heart's desire without let or hindrance.

Look for any small influence line between the milieu line and the fate line proper, for this intensifies the problems. The state of the fate line after the influence mark shows how well the subject has withstood the troublesome period.

A weakened line indicates things have got too much for him. If the line eventually tails off, the opposition has won. But if the line remains strong, the owner takes it in his stride.

There may be assorted small lines of milieu stemming from several different sources. The more there are, the less effect they seem to have, except for helping to fritter away everything. The subject is easily side-tracked.

A fate line with a forked starting point nearly always suggests inner conflict. When a branch from the mount of Venus meets with a branch from the Luna mount, the subject is well aware of what he is supposed to do regarding family wishes and personal ambitions.

The stronger of the two lines will show which effect wins in the end. There is almost always a sense of looking back, of what might have been. The clearer the line, the more success is likely, but this does not necessarily mean fame and fortune. The line shows how much real inner satisfaction the subject will enjoy through his efforts. Of course, if he makes money, and later becomes well known as a result, that is an added bonus.

When the line starts faintly then becomes quite strongly marked, the subject might have had a shaky initial start, but it would not have taken long to find the right input levels for him to have got into his stride.

A line from the Luna mount to the base of the Jupiter finger is always a sign of strong personal motivation. When the fate line blends in with the heart line, the aims have always been desired. The firmer the line, the more pronounced the trait.

When the fate line stops at the heart line with no other mark or influence line to be seen, an emotional error will have been responsible for the failure to realise ambitions. If the fate line stops at the head line, poor judgement is probably the reason for the failure. Should the fate line separate into several different branches just prior to any type of termination, a variety of reasons will be to blame e.g. the owner may become too embroiled or side-tracked to realise the path he is treading.

When the main fate line divides into many smaller lines between the heart and the head line, then similar events are quite likely to occur, although the various interests may be offshoots of the main ambition.

Sometimes, the fate line forks and sends one branch to the mount of Jupiter and one to Saturn. An important influence has caused this change of direction. Where the fork starts will show the origin of this. If at the head line, it may have been a business consideration: at the heart line, it shows it was always the aim anyway and the subject felt it was time to make the change.

When the line separates into several smaller lines, or forks into two, three or more branches, the reasons for where they lead to or stop are easily determined. For example, when a line goes to Jupiter with a secondary branch to Mercury, it could be a medical or business matter: Mercury and Saturn linked suggest a study in their associated fields of interest. If Apollo and Saturn were to be linked, entertainment matters are a possibility – the list is endless.

Traditionally, a line with a triple fork at its ending is said to be extremely fortunate. Up to a point this is only so when one of the forks end at the head line, heart line and the Jupiter or Apollo mounts.

The fate line that starts at the wrist and rises straight to the base of the middle finger marks the subject as a fatalist. Such folk always have what seems to be an inescapable sense of duty. If their life is in a rut, they do nothing to try to make things any better because they feel it is their lot and put up with it. Intermittent lines that fade and return show some attempts have been made to pursue something, but it has been to no avail.

When a fate line starts between the head and the heart lines, it shows a long-nurtured ambition that the subject has been unable to follow has finally taken off. If the line begins between the heart line and the base of the fingers, the subject has dreamed of the idea for many a long year.

The fate line that begins from the heart line shows that a hobby or other spare-time interest that long fascinated the owner eventually became part of the career. This may be verified by a loop in the skin pattern that enters the palm between the second and third fingers – the loop of serious intent.

If the fate line should end in the rarely seen Ring of Saturn, a line around the base of the medius, the subject will be obsessed with his career or ambitions to the exclusion of all else. His personality and character will be marked by a single-mindedness and drive that can override all other considerations.

Strictly speaking, there is no sense of time as far as the fate line is concerned. That there is a beginning is agreed, and this is from the base of the hand upward.

Where the fate line crosses the head line is about the thirty-fifth year, and where the heart and fate lines meet is approximately the fiftieth year mark. Develop a question-and-answer technique to establish a sense of timing events properly.

Never underestimate the importance of this line, whether it is in the hand or not. If it is not there, the subject can be likened to a loose cannon, for there is no sense of direction. But when it is found, it must be given a very careful examination and assessment every time.

20
The Minor Lines

In previous chapters on the main lines, references were made to the minor lines or influence marks, but without offering more complete explanations. There are a variety of these lesser lines and markings. Some are seen quite often while others are rarely – if ever – noted.

When suddenly confronted with a palm bearing a vast complexity of lines, a student may think it is virtually impossible to discern anything. Such a fine tracery may not all be influence marks, but definite minor lines that can be identified.

However, before we even try to delineate them individually, the overall picture should be assessed first. Where hands *and* lines are concerned, there are three types – the full, empty or average.

The Full Hand
The full hand means exactly that. It is easy to recognise because there is a vast complexity of lines crisscrossing the surface of the palm. It is always an indication of a worrier.

People with markings like this are never still. Their mind cannot switch off when it should. They simply do not know when to let go of a problem, even after it has been resolved. Over-emotional and highly strung, such types possess the most vivid imagination.

Generally speaking, these folk are basically unhappy because it is not easy for them to trust the motives of others and they worry about upsetting people around them. As a result, they always seem to live on a knife-edge.

They are far from being overly negative souls. Many can – and do – have brilliant minds and lead fascinating lives. Perceptive and understanding, many reach the top early, but few manage to stay the course.

Those who do so only remain at the top because of the ability to impress individuals who matter. When under pressure, they tend to get restless and ill at ease, and are unable to carry things through.

The Empty Hand

The opposite of this is the empty hand. It has just the three or four main lines, and perhaps two or three minor markings. The hand looks empty: the owner may seem devoid of feelings.

These people have a steadier, more reliable approach and are able to assume responsibility with ease. Relatively free from worries and troubles, little gets them down and they do not feel things as acutely as the full hand.

Such people do not often show their feelings as they prefer not to display emotional involvement with anyone, especially in public places. As a rule, there is a very strong tenacity of purpose, but limited to what is important for them. These folk are noted for their thoroughness.

Once their mind is made up, they continue quietly and confidently until the task is completed – properly. Largely conventional and straightforward, they leave their mark when necessary.

The Average Hand

The average hand is the mean between the full and the empty hand, but it is often quite hard to be sure to which category it belongs.

When a palm obviously has more lines than an empty hand but somehow does not quite look like a full hand, classify it as average.

A good way to make sure is to check if there are more vertical lines than horizontal. Vertical lines show that the owner makes continuous concerted efforts to better his conditions and little gets in his way. Horizontal lines across the palmar surface are signs of obstructions, largely due to the interference of other people.

The Sun Line

The Sun line can start almost anywhere on the ulna or outer side of the palm and should follow a path to the centre of the mount of Apollo.

It can begin from the wrist and follow a similar path to the fate line, if there is one. Often called the Apollo line because of where it ends, it is also known as the line of brilliance, fame, fortune or success.

Despite all this, the line does not confer brilliance and should not be regarded as pointing to success. However, it does confer a talent for hard work no matter how it is formed, and the owner is only really happy when stretched to the full.

There is an innate talent for getting the best out of others and they earn the respect of those around them. Others admire these types for what they do and what they are.

The later the start of the line, the more determined the nature, especially when it begins from the head line. If the line starts from the heart line, these subjects need to rely on the encouragement of others close to them.

When the fate line and a Sun line appear together, always look to see which is the stronger. If the fate line is stronger, the nature is more serious and may lack spontaneity. But if the Sun line is the stronger of the two, the personality is far more outgoing and uninhibited.

When there is no Sun line, especially in the hand of a successful person, the owner feels there are few limits to his talents and ambitions. He may think he is infallible and firmly believes in his own publicity. If this type falls from grace, they do so with a very loud bang indeed!

The Girdle of Venus

This may be a single line or a series of small interlinked lines, chains or islands between the heart line and the top of the hand just below the base of the fingers. It always signifies extreme emotional sensitivity because it lies along the emotional part of the hand.

One single line is rather unfortunate. The owner rarely enjoys a quiet or peaceful emotional nature, suffers heightened emotional sensitivity and is always on the look-out for fresh stimulation.

This character is easily bored, cannot sustain concentration for long and is too easily side-tracked. One sign of this particular formation is nervous excitability, rather like a child who never really grows up.

The single line Girdle is not often seen, and when it is, it often appears on one hand only. The more broken the Girdle, the less sensitive the emotional nature, and the more common sense prevails. But this character must still be able to get an emotional charge from somewhere or something. Also associated with the Girdle is fastidiousness, which can often be carried to extremes.

The Via Lasciva

A person's need for physical stimulation or excitement is always shown when this line is present. There are two distinct positions in which it may be found.

It will either appear as a small semi-circular line linking the base of the mount of Venus with that of the Lunar mount or can be seen as a sister line to the Mercury line. It may appear as one single line, be broken, chained or islanded much like the Girdle, with which it is often linked. In essence, its appearance can – and does – vary considerably, even on one pair of hands.

The line that links the two mounts in the physical part of the hand shows the owner constantly seeks physical stimulation to offset what he or she may feel is a boring, routine life.

When the Via Lasciva is found inside the life line, the subject will go to extreme lengths to satisfy this need. If the line is curved or twisted, it can lead to excesses involving drink, drugs or sex.

However, when this line is more of a straight link between the two mounts, it may be an allergy line. People with this marking are often sensitive to certain foods, drugs or drink and have learned to avoid them. This kind of allergy or aversion to certain foodstuffs may be linked to the fatalist thinking of medieval times, when this was known as the poison line.

When the Via Lasciva acts as a sister line to the Mercury line, it conveys much the same message, but here it seems linked with those who prefer a natural way of life, vegetarianism, people who avoid drugs in favour of natural medicines.

When the Girdle of Venus and the Via Lasciva are both present in the hand, make sure the head line is strong enough to fight the temptations or give way to them. A strong line on a firm hand helps to counteract the problem, but a weak line on a soft hand can help accentuate the weaknesses.

The Mercury Line
This line has many names and is known variously as the Hepatica, the health line, business line, line of intuition, liver line or the stomach line.

This line may start at the base of the hand near or on the life line, or just inside it, from the mount of Neptune, or the Luna mount.

Sometimes, it can begin anywhere in the zone of Mars or from just above the end of the head line if that line reaches that far. As a rule, the line ends on the mount of Mercury, but does not always do so.

It is better for it not be present in the hand, for then there is little concern with health matters. When found, it does not matter how it is formed or, within reason, where it is located on the passive side of the hand. It will always refer to a lasting or recurring health problem of some kind.

The line reflects hidden wants, needs, fears and basic desires. Thus, when present it suggests the subject is aware of his subconscious system in some way. But whether this refers to the nervous, sympathetic, intuitive or automatic responses depends on supportive evidence from elsewhere.

If the line stems from the life line, the owner is actively aware of health matters. He may be always on a diet, but not necessarily because of weight problems. It could be because he has medically to maintain a balanced intake of vitamins. This is another sign of a fastidious nature.

If the line begins inside the life line, there could be a digestive weakness, and the more the line twists or turns, the stronger the implication. When the line starts from the zone of Mars, there may still be an interest in health and associated matters, but expect to find some business ability as well.

The zone of Mars is concerned with mundane affairs. When the Mercury line starts here, the owner has an instinctive aptitude for business matters.

Line of Intuition

If the line begins low on the Luna mount and moves inward and upward in a semi-circular path to the outer edge of the hand to end on the negative Mars mount or even the Mercury mount, it is called the line of Intuition.

It is rarely present as a continuous line, but often islanded, chained or full of breaks. When seen, it suggests prescience, and the clearer the line, the stronger the inner sixth sense.

If the line should cross the head line in both hands, the subject will demonstrate practical ability and a natural interest in all occult matters. If the head line forks and this line crosses both branches, it is a sign of hyper-sensitivity.

Should the line form a triangle with the lines of head and fate, it is considered as a mark of clairvoyance. If the line merges at the end with the Medical Stigmata, the owner will be involved in healing in one form or another.

The Simian Line

Strictly speaking, this is a fusion of the head and heart lines into one

THE MINOR LINES

single line across the palmar surface. As a rule, this line tends to be set low on the palm which, in turn, implies an emotional imbalance.

The owner has a very intense outlook on life. He loves and hates with dramatic fervour. He is egocentric, wrapped up in his own world to the exclusion of all else. This type believes the world exists for him and him alone. He has tremendous powers of concentration and employs them for his own ends in such a way he that he can appear utterly ruthless to others.

It is a mixture of the emotional capacity and the intellectual ability. The higher it is on the hand, the more emotion rules: the lower the line, the more intellect takes over. Either way, once the owner decides to pursue a course of action, his whole being is swept up in the need to achieve that aim.

If found on the left hand only the owner tends to react quite emotionally if something should go wrong. One day, this character is drastic and severe while the next day he is liable to exhibit an almost cloying sentimentality. It is rarely possible to predict which way the moods will go.

When on the right hand only, expect to find a Jekyll and Hyde personality. Mostly, the owner is aware of this, but instead of trying to control himself in a proper manner, he is more likely to capitalise on it and work everything to his favour.

These people do not constantly display extremes of behaviour. In fairness, folk with the Simian line usually behave normally most of the time and should always be treated as though they do.

The Sydney Line
Occasionally, a normal head line crosses straight over the middle of the palm and appears to cut the hand in two. This indicates a personality whose mental powers control all his responses, even if the line slopes a little. This is called the Sydney line and shows somebody whose mental strength can – and does – override all emotional considerations if deemed necessary, irrespective of any other contradictory line formation.

The heart line is often quite faint in comparison. If found on both hands, the nature can be compared to that produced by the Simian line.

Travel Lines
There are several places where travel lines may be found, but in

general those on the mount of the Moon are the most favourable.

A number of lines are often seen to enter the palm from the outer edge of the hand on the lower part of the Luna mount. These lines must be clear of any influences, breaks or other marks. If this is the case, they show journeys safely made. If the line turns upward, travel is successful: if they turn downward, the journey can be fraught with problems.

A star on the end of such a line suggests a profitable outcome. A square traditionally shows protection from danger while the circle is a warning sign of danger through drowning. Meanwhile, a triangle is regarded as mark of profit through experience and often seen on the hands of students who travel abroad to further their education.

Another sign of a love of travel is when the life line ends on the mount of the Moon or sends a branch to it. There is always a love of travel with wide palms or widely spaced fingers and a forked line of head, but this is more restlessness than a desire for actual travel.

The Rascettes

These are two, three or possibly four or more lines found at the base of the palm where the wrist meets the hand proper. In oriental hand reading, it was traditionally thought the bracelets were linked with longevity, but there is very little to support or contradict this.

Sometimes, the top line arches up into the base of the palm. On a woman's hand it can indicate possible difficulties with her urinogenital system. It might be anything from the bladder to menstrual problems. Should the second line arch into the palm as well, the weakness will be aggravated.

Lines of Restlessness

Restlessness may be marked by a series of small lines that enter the palm from the outer edge of the hand below the heart line. This is a sign of those who dislike being inactive. If the marks are deeply etched this will be accentuated.

This type thrives on being in the centre of things and is often the backbone of small local societies or other groups.

Frustration Lines

Many small horizontal lines on the lower phalange of the fingers are signs of frustration. In particular, the finger on which they are seen indicates the probable source of the annoyance.

If found on the Mercury finger, problems in business matters, communications or travel are likely. When observed on the Apollo finger, there will be difficulties related to the creative arts.

On the Saturn finger, it may be relationship difficulties while on the Jupiter finger it suggests that the owner's ambitions or religious convictions could be the source of the problem. If seen on all of the fingers, the subject dislikes and is unable to cope with stress and strain.

Lines of Stress and Strain

Vertical lines running the entire length of the finger phalanges always indicate stress. A fluffy look to the head line shows the owner suffering stress for as long as the fluffiness is present.

The so-called white lines that appear across the top phalange of the fingers always show stress, which is usually generated by the owner overdoing things. This character tends to burn candles at both ends ... and the body can only take so much. However, a good meal and adequate rest normally restore the status quo.

Of course, we must not forget that bitten nails are recognisable danger signals – outward signs of inner stress and strain. When seen with these lines of irritation, they accentuate the problem.

There are five rings or small lines that encircle the base of the four fingers and the thumb. These few very small lines are not often encountered.

The Ring of Jupiter

Also known as the ring of Solomon, this small line curves around the base of the first finger near or at the top of the mount. It confers wisdom and the ability to teach or impart knowledge. It also gives an air of authority, so the combination of these gifts can make the owner well respected in this environment.

The Ring of Saturn

The path of this line around the base of the middle finger has the effect of cutting off the balancing influence of the finger on the rest of the hand. There is little openness or spontaneity in the make-up. It often symbolises the lone-wolf type.

The Ring of Apollo

This ring has a decided two-fold effect. On a poor hand, it shows poor taste, bad decisions and a lack of artistic appreciation. On a well formed hand, it indicates the dedicated or specially gifted public figure.

However, it is also a warning. In the event of an "incident", this person will fall from grace with much adverse publicity.

The Ring of Mercury

Once again, there is a traditional meaning and a more modern one. Traditionally, it is the sign of the true bachelor or spinster, one to whom marriage has little to offer, although they do enjoy normal relationships with members of the opposite sex. It is *not* a sign of homosexuality!

The modern interpretation suggests business ability, but often at the expense of relationships. As an employer, this character can be quite ruthless. It is rarely in the hands of subordinates, for they cannot stand being ordered around.

The Family Ring

This line is a regular feature in the hand, for it is the dividing mark between the second phalange of the thumb and the mount of Venus.

This line does not have a cutting effect like the all the other digital rings. As a rule, it is a chained formation and in some hands strongly marked while hardly seen in others.

The heavily etched line shows very strong ties between the owner and the rest of the family. Influence lines that cross the mount of Venus from the family ring refer to matters entirely within the family circle.

If they cross the life line, the family influence will always be apparent in whatever the owner says or does.

The Loyalty Line

One or two very strong lines from the mount of Venus that stem from, but do not actually touch, the family ring indicate intense family loyalty either as a whole or for one or more individuals within the family.

If the lines touch the ring, the loyalty will be fanatical with the family name and honour always being considered first. This does not necessarily refer to a blood relationship, but to the domestic circle in which the owner was raised and he or she regards as family.

21
Special Marks and Signs

There are a wide variety of special marks likely to appear almost anywhere on the hand, the palmar surface, the back of the hand, on the front, back or side of the fingers and, of course, in among all the lines.

These special marks and signs are the bar, chain, circle, cross, dot, grille, island, square, star, tassel, triangle, trident, and vertical or horizontal lines.

They can appear singly or be connected with a line or lines with other marks that could have been accidentally formed through the random conjunction of major or minor lines.

Generally speaking, the circle, square, star, triangle, trident and vertical line are all considered to be fortunate and often found on the mounts. All other configurations – the bar, chain, cross, dot, grille, island and tassel – indicate negative values dependent on where they are found.

The Bar
Any obstruction on a line stops the flow of energy of that line. If it seems to be weaker after the interruption, the problem it represents has left its mark and will always be remembered. As a rule, the bar indicates a delay in the plans of the subject.

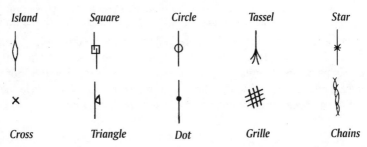

Some commonly seen small signs and special marks, but not every hand has them all. They can – and do – appear or fade away very quickly.

112

The Chain

A chain formation looks like a series of small connected islands and always shows a weakening of the power of the line on which it is found. Mostly, it points to a weakened constitution within the context of the line in which it is located.

On the life line, it might be the general physical well-being. On the heart line, the vascular system may be under par or it could refer to an emotional problem: the owner has trouble keeping and maintaining relationships. On the head line, it shows an inability to concentrate for long spells while physically it might mean a period of poor health related to an injury to the head or neck.

The Circle

This is a comparatively rare mark, and to be sure it is a circle it must not touch a line, but stand on its own. Wherever it is found, it is largely beneficial, but there are three exceptions.

On the lower part of the Luna mount it is traditionally a sign of danger of death through drowning. If on or next to the heart line under the third finger or if found on the inner side of the life line, the subject may experience sight problems.

On the Jupiter mount the circle is a symbol of practical success through learning whereas on the Apollo mount it indicates the owner has natural talents to help him win through. If on the Saturn mount, the circle reflects good investigative powers while on the Mercury mount a circle suggests a flair for business matters.

The Cross

The cross is made by two opposing lines of energy: a crossroads. Almost without exception it is regarded as an unlucky sign. If something goes wrong, it is beyond the owner's control. The cross says, "Stop, look and listen".

When any part of a cross touches a line it weakens its power. If a line ends in a cross, the change it brings can be quite drastic, a complete reversal of fortune.

A cross – or crosses – are often found on the nail phalange of the middle finger, usually at the side. A quite clearly etched cross is said to show a love of animals. If poorly formed, it presages danger from them.

The Dot
Basically, the dot can only appear on a line, so it may be taken as representing a temporary interference to its power, usually a delaying effect.

The Grille
Try to envisage the grille as a collection of crosses where all the criss-crossing lines permanently oppose one other. Every good indication is undone by bad aspects. Little can really come of anything no matter how hard the subject tries.

In essence, it indicates a dissipation of power. This is almost always found on the mount of Venus and implies weakened physical resources in non-productive activities or futile pursuits.

It weakens resolve. The owners begin projects, but rarely manage to finish what they start. Any line that ends in a grille has the same meaning. People who have grille formations here work better under direct supervision.

On the mount of Jupiter, a grille shows a cold and selfish nature. When on the Saturn mount, the subject lacks real direction: such folk rarely have properly thought out plans. If seen on the Apollo mount it indicates vanity and fallibility – these people tend to suffer from delusions of adequacy.

A grille on the Mercury mount shows a devious nature, someone who sets out to deceive others and profit by it. Unfortunately for him, most people see through the scheme so the subject cannot win no matter how hard he or she tries.

A grille on the mount of the Moon indicates an unhealthy attitude because the owner has a distorted imagination. There is little or no attempt to control the extremes to which the mind may go. If the health line travels through a grille, it greatly enhances the imaginative senses and leads to nervous excitability and temper tantrums.

Should the head line end in a grille it suggests a loss of mental control at the end of life. A grille on the second phalange of the thumb implies inability to make decisions, someone who does not take all the factors into account. There may also be a strong degree of self-deception in the make-up.

The Island
Islands can only appear on a line and are not a favourable mark. They weaken the strength and resolve of the line on which they are found.

When the life line creates an island, it weakens the constitution, implying delicacy and poor health for as long as the line is divided. If the line tasselates afterwards or seems to fray, especially at the end, physical health is likely to weaken accordingly.

If the line of life begins with an island, or islands, it shows a weakly child or one with poor enthusiasm or little zeal for life. If the line strengthens, so does the health. If the line begins as an open-ended island, there may be some mystery or a difficulty attached with the actual birth. In some cases there can be doubted parentage.

When the heart line begins as an open-ended island, it implies a hereditary health fault or family weakness, possibly linked with the heart or vascular system.

An island on either the fate or the Sun lines tends to weaken the direction and resolve of the subject. It becomes harder to pursue ambitions, and the career suffers a set-back or a series of them. If either line ends in an island formation, misfortune and losses will occur.

The mental functions cannot perform properly for as long as there is an island present within the head line. A head line that ends in an island (not a fork) shows deteriorating mental abilities as life comes to a close.

An island in the health line is equally as unhelpful as having the line present in the first place. Thus, it aggravates the problems suggested by the general formation of the line. When the health line ends in an island, or a series of small islands, it suggests the way life may end. The utmost tact and diplomacy will be needed when this configuration is seen here.

The Square

Wherever it is seen, the square is always favourable. It may be a specific formation or can occur accidentally as lines cross one another.

Mostly, it is recognised as a sign of preservation. If it covers a break in a line, the owner survives the problem safely. Should the line look strong and healthy after a square, recovery can be expected with little lasting affect.

A properly formed individual square on a mount protects the owner from excesses represented by the the mount. However, when a square is found on the Jupiter mount it is called the teacher's square. It shows an ability to instruct, to pass on knowledge – the mark of a natural teacher.

On the Saturn mount, a square helps to maintain a healthy overall balance in life while a square on the Apollo mount shows that tradition plays a large part in the subject's general outlook. A square on the Mercury mount confers good communication abilities.

A properly formed square just inside but not touching the line of life on the mount of Venus indicates a part of life spent away from others. It might be hospitalisation, perhaps a monastic or convent life, possibly prison in some cases. An examination of the rest of the hand should show which possibility.

The Star

The star denotes an intensification of the energy relating to the area or line upon which it is found. Made up of a concentration of many small lines meeting at one central point, the energies converging all at once must be something of a shock to the system. The effect is never forgotten.

On the life line, a star indicates physical shock or injury; on the head line a severe mental shock; on the heart line it implies a serious emotional shock or a possible heart attack.

If all three major lines have branches which converge together to meet in a star formation, the subject's lifestyle will be dramatically altered. Any people involved in this incident are never forgotten, no matter what part they may have played.

A star on the end of the fate or Sun lines suggests the career could end in brilliance or total disaster. This configuration is a clear sign that the owner is fully aware he or she lives their life permanently on a tightrope. They gamble all the time between the glory of fame and the dangers of infamy – a wager often lost in tragic circumstances.

The Tassel

A line may break into many small branches like a tassel at the end of curtain cord, and is usually seen toward the end of the life and health lines. It indicates a weakening of the energy of the line in old age. If seen on another line, it shows how the powers of that line naturally dissipate with age.

The Triangle

The problem with the triangle is that students may mistake it for a badly constructed square ... and these two shapes could not be more different.

The triangle is always favourable and shows an original, creative talent concerned with the area in which it is found. If next to a line, it enhances its power as long as it does not touch it in any way.

On the Jupiter mount, it confers tact and diplomacy while on the mount of Saturn it suggests research work, perhaps with secrecy involved. A triangle on the mount of Apollo implies a practical artistic career like a sculptor, masseur or body-builder. The lower down the mount, the more practical the subject.

A triangle on the Mercury mount is a sign of politics, debating and social awareness: a wheeler-dealer of and with people. The owner is perceptive and has a natural talent for many varying elements of business. It also implies early leadership, for such people are noticed by those who matter and they open the door to promotion.

On the Venus mount, a triangle indicates a restraining influence in emotional expression. Where others may allow their passions to overwhelm them this suggests that reason, caution and reserve will rule. On the mount of Neptune, a triangle helps the subject to enjoy his natural intuition and there may even be psychic powers.

A triangle anywhere in the zone of Mars indicates a fighting and undaunted spirit. These people do not acknowledge set-backs, but come back fighting for what they think is rightfully theirs.

The Trident

Rarely seen, this mark has always been considered important in eastern palmistry but we in the west only notice it when a line ends in a clear three-pronged fork. It is accepted as a sign of success and good fortune associated with where it is found.

Single Vertical Lines

Vertical lines found on a full hand show how the subject views life by how many there are compared with the amount of horizontal lines present.

All vertical lines show a special effort made by the subject in relation to wherever they are located. However, horizontal lines suggest the reverse, for they are seen to act as an obstruction.

22
How to Time Events

The single most difficult exercise in palmistry is learning how to time events accurately. In the very early days, proper timing was virtually non-existent. Any success was the result of pure guess-work or a very lucky shot if things did occur as predicted.

Those people who were involved in the middle of the 19th century chirological revival never really seriously paid attention to it with the same zeal they put into their interpretation studies.

However, a number of different schemes were hatched by an almost equal number of palmists who thought they had hit on the right system. Fifty years ago it was a common cry that timing was still a problem and, as the 21st century dawns, the problem is still with us. If the truth were known, it is just as complex an affair as it was a hundred or five hundred years ago.

Of the many systems of which I am aware, almost all have some merit in them, but those selected for inclusion here need to be carefully studied before they are put into practice.

The easiest mistake to make is to assume that all hands are the same size which, of course, they are not. Hands are long or short, wide or narrow, and allowances must be made not only for this, but also for the lines that appear on them.

For example, a long life line on a long palm can easily extend to the end of the skin pattern near the wrist. But it can also do so on a short hand. On a short hand, the short line of life may only reach halfway down the palm, but it also happens on a long palm.

The traditional suggestion that length of the line of life should correspond with three score years and ten no longer holds water. This thinking has evolved from the bible, and nobody has questioned it.

In the 1950s, life expectancy for a man was around 61 years. The latest study tells us it is now nearer 85 years whilst women live a little longer. Thus, the concept of the life line as representing 70 years has always been wrong, but perhaps never more so than today.

Experience shows that common sense must prevail with individual hands every time. Perhaps then the golden rule for determining times and dates will become much easier to define.

One aspect is absolutely certain – it is not possible to date any event by specifically naming a day, date, or time. Any claims of this nature must viewed with suspicion as it just cannot be done.

Time on the Nails

We know we are able to measure time reasonably accurately on the nails because the ridges that refer to ill-health can be measured to within two or three weeks quite easily. On average, it takes a nail about 180 days to grow out fully, so one with an indent half-way along would have begun to grow about 90 days earlier.

With careful measurement, one ought to be able to determine the start of a period of poor health to within a week or two at the very least. When other nails bear similar marks of confirmation timing becomes much easier.

Time on the Life Line

Take a small length of twine or cotton and lay it on the subject's life line. Try to be as precise as you can. Cut the material at the end of the line and fold it exactly in half. Place it back on the beginning of the line again.

Where the material now ends represents age 35–40. Mark this point lightly on the hand itself (or print) then divide the material in half and repeat the exercise again. Where the material ends this time gives an approximate age of eighteen to twenty. Repeat this and the new point is roughly nine to ten years of age.

If you carry out the same exercise on the lower half of the line you will be able to time events for the latter part of the life just as easily. Incidentally, this method may be safely used with both the fate and Sun lines, but using the timing system for those lines, of course.

A second method that produces good results consists of what seems to be drawing imaginary lines on the palm. From the middle of the base of the first finger draw a line straight down to the line of life and where it intersects is at about age ten or so.

From the beginning of the life line to this point represents the first ten years of life. It does help to establish a dialogue with your subject because a question-and-answer system soon establishes the accuracy of the scheme which, if it is initially correct, allows you to continue along the same lines.

A second line drawn from between the first and second fingers to the life line cuts in around age twenty or so. A third line taken from the bottom of the finger of Saturn to the life line crosses at about age 35–36.

Beyond this, unfortunately, the system fails should the line not reach this far out into a palm. Nevertheless, if all the earlier experiments worked it becomes quite easy to gauge events on the rest of the line. Remember that whatever system you use there are other lines on which time may be estimated and you should try to interpret them together.

Once satisfied you have found the middle point of the life line, it will go a long way to establishing important dates on the second half of the line. However, following on from what was said earlier regarding life expectancy, the timing of events using any of these methods could be out by quite a lot. Now perhaps you appreciate the difficulty that modern hand readers have when they come to apply these old formulas today.

Despite all the modern research currently carried out, until we find something more accurate to work with, this is all we have. For the time being, we must make do with the best we can. As an afterthought, what does not help a lot is that some hand analysts find these time scales are equally as accurate if they begin their timing estimations where traditionalists end theirs. Readers are invited to experiment.

Time on the Fate Line
When this line is long enough to end at the base of the middle finger or on the mount of Saturn, the point where it crosses the head line represents age 35–36 and when it goes over the heart line is roughly age 45–50.

Take the length from the base of the hand to the head line and divide it equally into three. Each section may then be said to represent ten or twelve years. A similar dating system may be used on the Sun line, but in this case remember to make your calculations to and from the mount of Apollo, the normal ending for this line.

Time on the Head Line

The timing of events on this line often proves to be difficult, but if a section of the fate line intersects it the exercise is much easier.

The first half of the head line, from under the first finger to where the fate line crosses it (or would do so if long enough) represents age 35–36. The second half of the line now equals from age 35–36 to age 70.

Once again, there are those who would read the timing of events on this line from the percussion to the radial side of the hand.

Time on the Heart Line

Irrespective of where the heart line begins on the radial side of the hand, draw an imaginary line from the middle of the base of the first finger toward the bottom of the hand and then another line from the base of the little finger downward.

Where the first of these lines cross the heart line is roughly age ten, and the second point about age 70. It does not matter if these points do not tally with the beginning and ending of the heart line itself. The mid-point of the intersections is taken to be read as age 35–36.

Once again, there are two schools of thought. There are those who prefer to have the heart line begin on the radial side and others who claim it starts at the percussion.

Yet another school of thought suggests that because of what the line represents time cannot be read on this line. They, too, have a valid point because if you think about it, you cannot really date matters on this line unless you are trying to gauge health matters.

However, all these suggestions have worked in practice and will do so as long you remember to use a time scale longer than the traditional 70 years. Adjust accordingly.

Part Three
DERMATOGLYPHICS
The Skin Patterns

23
The Digital Patterns

It is now fully appreciated that the patterns of fine ridges and furrows on the hand's palmar surface remain constant throughout life.

They cannot be erased or destroyed unless, of course, disturbed by accident or injury. Skin patterns do, however, break up during illness and poor health, but once the subject recovers they resume their normal appearance.

A curious and little-known fact is that these markings are, in some cases, the only form of identification after death. They can still be detected long after other features have deteriorated.

Skin patterns are formed in the few months of foetal life and remain unchanged. Composed of tiny ridges and furrows called capillary lines, they stretch from all the outer edges of the palmar surface to the tips of the fingers. Although everyone has different finger and palmar prints, there are quite definite patterns.

It is not known exactly when man first noticed these formations, although many references have been made to them down the centuries. Thousands of years ago, in China deals and agreements were "sealed" by palmar or thumb imprints.

As similar uses were made of these highly personal markings in Europe and many Middle Eastern countries, we know that not only did these cultures appreciate their individuality and singular method of identification, but used them as proof of it.

There are two quite distinct patterns. One appears small, with a fine "closed" look and is composed of small but delicately marked tiny ridges and furrows that are almost indecipherable. The other type is open and "wide" in comparison. All the ridges and furrows may be easily traced without the aid of a magnifying glass because the pattern is so bold.

The finely textured line and pattern formations indicate the naturally refined and rather gentle types who exhibit inherent sensitivity in all they say or do. The overall approach is mental, their actions and reactions determined by the mind. These characters are less physical than the other other type.

The wider textured skin pattern shows a person with an open mind, one who has a somewhat physical personality. Materialistic, down-to-earth and practical, they think direct action is the best avenue to pursue and their instincts are to live along these lines. They are not necessarily less intelligent, but tend to have a limited imagination at times.

The fingerprint types

There are five distinct fingerprint patterns – the arch, composite, loop, tented arch and whorl. Like other features in the hand, there are occasional variations.

To view them properly, you need a reasonably powerful magnifying glass. However, it is much easier to take prints. You can use almost any medium you like for this, from a stamp pad to a lipstick, but the most effective is a water-based ink, which is also the easiest to clean off afterwards (see the chapter on taking prints).

The Arch pattern
The arch pattern is quite basic. It looks like a simple bridge. This, in turn, tends to reflect the subject's personality traits because in much the same way as you trust a bridge so, too, can you trust those with the basic arch pattern.

They are capable and reliable people who, when things go wrong, are able to cope extremely well. They may lack subtlety and tend to take life a trifle too seriously. These folk are often suspicious of others' motives and may seem guarded or intractable, perhaps with a slightly repressed emotional outlook.

The expression "salt of the earth" sums them up well, but make no mistake: they are not fools and should not be treated as such, for they make loyal friends, and good employees and employers. If their trust is breached in any way, they are very unforgiving.

The index finger
An arch on the first finger suggests realism. These people thrive well

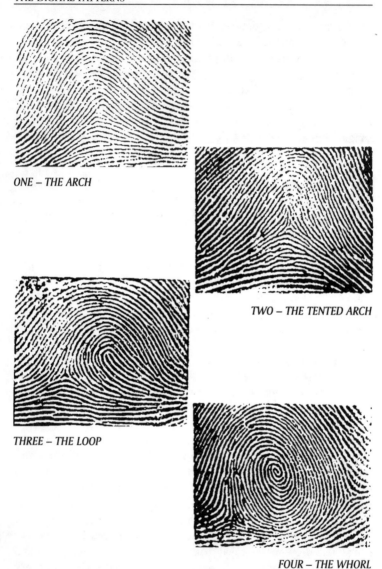

ONE – THE ARCH

TWO – THE TENTED ARCH

THREE – THE LOOP

FOUR – THE WHORL

*There are four basic patterns: the arch, tented arch, loop and whorl.
Everyone has them, one way or another, but not as perfect as
these illustrations. There are many variations.*

in a position of power and authority. They can be slow starters, but finish what they begin.

The middle finger
An arch pattern here indicates an ability to improve things wherever they may be. On a square hand, it suggests a do-it-yourself enthusiast. Emotional expression is not easy for them. They could be slightly inhibited.

The third finger
This adds a somewhat practical approach to creative and artistic inclinations. Abstract art does not appeal. Such types have a far more constructive or practical outlook.

The fourth finger
As a rule, an arch on the fourth finger is one of a set or a part of the dominant pattern on both hands. There will be a practical turn of mind and hand in the way these people communicate. Change does not always attract or appeal, but such folk soon catch on.

The thumb
This implies a good sense of self-preservation and is, quite often, a strong overriding feature of the whole character. If found on a firm thumb, there will be plenty of common sense. If it is weak or the hand is soft, a lazy streak is indicated.

The Composite
It can be difficult precisely to define the composite pattern, for although it really belongs to the whorl family, it can be made up of almost any of the other patterns. Thus, it may be comprised of a loop and an arch, or a tented arch, a whorl and a loop, or even twin loops.

It is fairly rare, but now and again the composite, or compound, pattern may include lateral pockets and accidentals. These are occasional patterns which do not quite belong to any of the other categories.

From a chirological viewpoint, this mind is able to see both sides of any question because these subjects are always open to an opposing view or impression. They dislike accepting anything at face value and want to look at all the possibilities before committing themselves.

These folk prefer to experience things at first hand because they so dislike second-hand information or another's viewpoint. He or she is a materialist and can often seem unresponsive in emotional matters. They are not very flexible in personal relationships and can be quite difficult to live with.

The first finger

This is the mark of the planner, the schemer, the sort of person who is unable to make a firm decision or start anything without first thinking the whole thing through, by which time it is often too late. There can also be an inner conflict of ideals or ambitions.

The second finger

This suggests an extremely matter-of-fact attitude to just about anything and anyone. Once the mind is made up, nothing will shift the subject. He or she may have a strong career commitment.

The third finger

There is a basic down-to-earth approach to everything. The owner dislikes unnecessary frippery. Food has to be plain and simple; dress is conservative; artistic appreciation is basic. The nature is rather severe, with very limited tastes.

The fourth finger

People with this have difficulty in expressing their innermost feelings, so partners and friends can have their work cut out in trying to get along with or understand them. These individuals tend to be followers rather than leaders.

The thumb

The composite skin pattern suggests a hesitant, uncertain and rather slow response. These people work and play hard, although adaptability and flexibility are not their forte, and their tolerance levels are low. They do not enjoy really close relationships.

Here we should include the twin loop pattern. This is a rather rare occurrence, but when seen it suggests a "push-me, pull-you" kind of attitude. Emotional mood swings from one level to another can happen very quickly indeed. This intensity is always fairly evident. The subject has a tendency to volatile responses, but in all other respects his or her nature is fairly straightforward.

The lateral pocket pattern is usually composed of two loops, but there can be three or even more at times, all swirling around.

The Loop
There are two basic loop patterns: the radial and the ulna. The radial loop occurs when the pattern appears to start from the thumb, creates the loop and returns again toward the active side of the hand. The ulna loop starts at the percussion, throws the loop and returns back to the unconscious side of the hand again.

Radial loops are more frequently found on the index finger, but if they should appear on another finger it is most likely to be the third. They are more frequently found on the right hand whereas the ulna loop is seen more commonly on the left.

Generally speaking, radial loops are found on the hands of those who tend to be more self-assured and positive. Depending on the finger and the hand, this formation indicates adaptability and flexibility, but only as a personal choice. But if the owner so chooses, he can dig his heels in and little will budge him: he can be very stubborn indeed.

Subjects with the ulna loop are far less stubborn and more open to suggestion. They have the gift for adding little extra touches that transform from the mediocre to the brilliant, an aptitude that should always be actively encouraged.

These subjects prefer the status quo and do not like to buck the system. Peace, perhaps, but not necessarily at any price!

The first finger
A loop here indicates the ability to improvise and adapt to any new ideas and plans with ease. These characters make good leaders because it is rare for them not to join in and sweep up or make the tea if there is nobody else around to do it. They are quite flexible, thoughtful and straightforward.

The second finger
There is a dislike of expending too much energy in the pursuance of an aim, either in the career or spare time. Frank and open, they

oppose unfairness or injustice and will do their utmost to correct an obvious wrong. These folk may be shy or withdrawn when in company.

The third finger

These characters exist in the "now" of life at all times. They must have everything *now*. Uninhibited and ready and willing to flout convention – probably to shock others more than anything else – they will try anything once … and again if they like it!

The fourth finger

Hopelessly impulsive, these types tend to commit to almost anything, but without thinking. While not wittingly unreliable, they are often horrified when the full import of what they have said dawns on them. Clever, perceptive and with good communication skills, the longer or more pointed the tip, the better the level of expression.

The thumb

Unless the thumb is very strong, personal discipline is not easy. Adroit, impulsive and socially orientated, these subjects are affectionate and warm natured. If there are two ulna loops, diplomatic skills are good. Two radial loops create more assertiveness.

The Tented arch

This looks like an upright slim loop, straight up the phalange, but it can lean a little either way. This shows the enthusiast, the ever-young reformer whose mission is to set the world to rights.

However, these types are idealists and good at inciting others to action while they do very little. Not always known for their tact and diplomacy, they know how to turn on the charm to get their way. There is an innovative side to their nature.

The first finger

This suggests the owners live life to the full at all times and are to be found supporting all manner of causes and the trend of the moment. They often burn the candle at both ends in order always to be in thick of things.

The middle finger
This is often the sign of an idealist, perhaps to the exclusion of all other considerations. Once hooked on to a new interest, he or she can become obsessive about a new friendship, job, a romance, and so on.

The third finger
The arts often play a large part in life, although not necessarily as a performer. This indicates a good host or hostess, somebody who knows how to present his or her best side to the world and always appears properly dressed.

The fourth finger
This is a rare sign, but the tented arch found here signifies a good command of language, and the ability to express well, verbally or in writing. There is often a special gift regarding commercial or business affairs at which these folk excel and, of course, make money.

The thumb
Not known for their decisiveness or a direct approach, these folk work best in the fields of diplomacy and negotiation. They know how to mix well with anyone, anywhere, and are extremely adaptable. They rarely stay for long in any one place.

The Whorl
No matter where you find this pattern, the basic characteristics are originality and individualism. Frequently, these people are often so complex they may seem cold or off-hand in their dealings with others.

They can be inwardly lonely, for they find it difficult to make friends and are so obstinate. Once they make up their mind, they have a fixity of purpose second to none and are very ambitious. People with this formation have difficulty in delegating responsibility because they feel no one can do the job as well as them.

They may seem slow at times, but do not let that fool you: they have razor-sharp minds and can be very effective in action. They are often found in occupations that involve emergency situations.

The first finger
Extremely ambitious and not very adaptable, these folk have to be asked to do things, never told. Whatever they work at probably has a vocational leaning, something specialised, but of use to the community as a whole. Teaching comes naturally, but so does maintaining discipline. You will learn with this one!

The second finger
Good planning ability. These people enjoy research or investigative work, but nothing very specialised. They are likely to have religious feelings or be fascinated by the whole concept. It is rare for them to change their mind. They are not swayed by the opinions or rhetoric of others.

The third finger
This is the most likely place for a whorl and shows very strong individualism in respect of art, fashion or entertainment. If on both hands, the owner will be unconventional and individualistic. Emotions are kept on a tight rein: they will not wear their heart on their sleeve. Such types learn by experience.

The fourth finger
The owner is not easily influenced by what he hears or sees. He rather likes to be thought of as the power behind the throne and thrives in such a situation. He is selective in all he does and with whom he associates. His major weakness is that he can talk, and talk, and talk …

The thumb
Whorls are rarely found on a weak thumb, but when they do appear there will be a stubborn nature, someone with little regard for opposition. If the whorl is set low, the nature is decisive and intense, but if set high, politics may interest. The subject can sacrifice to achieve – and this can include relationships.

24
The Palmar Patterns

The capillary lines and furrows that make up the skin patterns on the palmar surface are no different to those on the fingers. As a rule, there are not so many variations. What is present are mostly loops and whorls, but just occasionally the arch or the tented arch may be seen.

The mounts
An apex is where certain skin patterns meet and look like little triangles, especially on the mounts. They are normally quite easy to find, except on the mount of Venus where it is very difficult to see anything properly.

To find the exact centre of a mount, look at the skin pattern and trace it carefully until you find the apex, which should be at a point somewhere below the base of the finger. This need not be exactly under the finger. In fact, few mounts are centrally placed. Sometimes, two fingers appear to "share" the same mount. At times, the Jupiter and Saturn mounts can seem to be like a large pad under these two fingers.

If the apex of the skin pattern is nearer the Jupiter finger, then it should be read as a Jupiter/Saturn mount. If nearer the Saturn finger, it ought to be judged as being a Saturn/Jupiter mount.

The Mercury mount is nearly always displaced toward the mount of Apollo finger and is often to be found sharing this pad beneath these two fingers. A comprehensive interpretation of the mounts is dealt with in the chapter on the mounts.

The precise nature of all the other palmar patterns and the many and various formations can be difficult to assess at first. The pattern may be only partly formed or difficult to detect because of other considerations like the grille, for example.

Other patterns
You may have to spend quite some time checking through the palmar surface trying to find what patterns are there to establish their role

SKIN PATTERN APICES

To locate the centre of a mount, trace the apex in the skin pattern. This central point is not always exactly under the finger – very few are.

in the overall character. A pattern could form part of a bold and wide-open system of ridges and furrows or may look finely textured in comparison with the rest of the hand.

The open and wide pattern suggests the owner has more of a material outlook and nature, someone whose reactions are likely to be physical. The close-textured formation implies a refined, gentle and sensitive approach to life. Take care not to confuse texture with consistency.

A firm consistency refers to a good physical constitution, the person who is always on the move and who rarely indulges a lazy streak. The soft, flabby hand invariably means physical laziness.

Texture refers to the appearance of the skin pattern, which will either be wide and open-looking or close and fine. While we always have a defined skin pattern of some kind on our finger and thumb tips, palmar patterns are completely different.

It is rare to find more than a few on any individual hand. Some people might have none at all, but this is rare. Equally, it may be a rare few who have all the patterns. It is here that it becomes important to interpret in the light of the rest of the hand. For example, where an appreciation of music is indicated it may not necessarily be classical. Nor does it follow that the subject is musically proficient himself, only that he appreciates the art and derives great pleasure from it.

The Rajah loop
This pattern enters the top of the hand between the base of the first and second fingers. It may be on one hand only or on both.

It always refers to qualities of leadership. On the right hand, the subject will strive very hard for a position in society and sets great store by achievement.

In the left hand only, it suggests that leadership abilities are inherent and come naturally, as a right in some cases.

Serious Intent
This loop enters the palmar surface between the middle and third fingers. It may be on one hand only or on both. It always shows a strong and serious intent of some kind. It could be a hobby or other interest that eventually dominates life. This is often the case if the fate line ends in or quite near the central core of the loop.

If on the left hand only, ambitions have to play a waiting game: the subject is prepared to wait for the right moment to put his plans into action. When seen on just the right hand, the owner will work steadily toward the desired aim with a concentrated effort.

Humour
This pattern enters the palmar surface between the base of the third and fourth fingers and always shows a sense of humour. The larger the loop, the more pronounced the owner's sense of fun. He or she is the first on the dance floor, or to get up and make a fool of themselves at a party.

A square look to the loop suggests a more refined approach while one that sweeps over to the mount of Apollo makes the subject sensitive to criticism. It does occasionally add a kind of sixth sense to the nature, which may be displayed in any number of ways.

Music
On the mount of Venus there may be three small loops. It might be difficult to trace anything on this mount because in almost all cases

it is completely covered in a complexity of lines, grilles and other configurations.

However, if all three are present there will be a strong interest in music, perhaps a definite practical ability. One only suggests a love of stringed instruments. If a loop enters the mount from the angle of time, an enjoyment of rhythm in music is accentuated – martial music or similar. The third pattern enters the mount from the base of the palm in an elongated loop.

Whether the other two are present or not, this accentuates a love of music, but does not imply ability. It suggests a "natural" ear. Even if the subject cannot play or compose, he or she may be quite knowledgeable.

Courage

A loop sometimes enters the hand from the radial edge of the palm between the thumb and the first finger inside the life line. The owners will always demonstrate courage of some kind, either in their nature or the way they face seemingly continuous uphill tasks.

If the loop persists all the way to the life line, it helps the fight against illness. If it goes to or touches the family ring it may have something to do with the family honour.

Green fingers

A loop that enters the skin pattern from the percussion side of the hand at the top of the Luna mount shows a special affinity with animals and nature. A sixth sense will play a large part in the life. There is an "awareness" for things that are not quite right.

Memory

Another loop might be seen a little further into the hand where the "noose" of the loop encompasses the head line. This is the loop of memory. It may touch, surround or appear to swim with the line. When the head line ends in this loop, it shows an excellent memory, perhaps even to total recall standard if found on both hands.

Travel

A loop can lie along the very base of the mount of the Moon that moves right over to the percussion edge of the hand. This suggests that travel will play a large part in the subject's life, although the appeal may be for just short distances. If found on both hands, more extensive forays – such as inter-continental travel – will be favoured.

Intuition

When a loop enters the palm on the mount of Neptune from the base of the hand, there will be a marked sixth sense, an "awareness" of life, a natural intuition.

The subject has an uncanny knack for doing all the right things at all the right times as if inwardly inspired. If the fate line starts from this loop, the owner will be a fatalist all his life.

If the life line ends in this loop, the subject's life may be given over to caring for others.

Emotional expression

Sometimes, a clear arch formation can be seen in the skin pattern immediately above the heart line below the mount of Mercury. This shows someone who finds it difficult to express or demonstrate acts of affection. These people dislike kissing or embracing in public, even if greeting after a long separation or saying goodbye.

There are a number of other patterns that occasionally appear on a hand for which the real meanings have yet to be found. In many cases, they also have yet to be named. If you would like to experiment, here are just a few.

A loop in the skin pattern may be seen to lie between the mounts of Venus and the Moon. It might swim with the line of life or not, and can be long or short.

It seems connected with carers – those who spend their lives (not just a working life) helping others less fortunate. They have a splendid ear for just listening to those who have a sympathetic side to their nature.

Sometimes, a whorl can be seen on the Luna mount. This seems to relate to those who have the ability totally to submerge their own character into a role they play. Thus, it may be in an actor or investigator's hand. In either case, the subject has to assume a different personality or character to achieve the aim.

The "open field" on the Luna mount – a plain pattern with no loops, arches or other formations – seems to belong to those who are free from worry and complexes, and is often found on the hands of those who live in rural areas. Nothing bothers them. They call a spade a spade and are content within themselves.

Even if the lines should refer to problems, these people cope well under stressful conditions. Some authorities suggest this is because they could have limited understanding, but perhaps as they live so close to nature, such folk are more prone to take a natural and simple course to solve their problems.

Handprints

Building a library of prints for permanent reference is not hard work and can be great fun. However, you need to create an easy-to-follow system that is also simple to maintain. Without doubt, the best and easiest recording procedure is the alphabetic.

You should write data on the reverse of your prints or you can use a simple 128 x 76 mm record card (5" x 3") so that damage to prints is kept to a minimum. Information regarding the physical hand that would not normally be seen on a print, such as the colour, texture, nail details and other facts, may then be filed safely away.

Of course, if you have a computer, so much the better. These days they all have a built-in database somewhere in their system and can be used to cross-reference data with enormous speed.

Keeping records and handprints for reference must never be under-estimated because as permanent records they are an essential part of hand analysis.

Most interview sessions are limited by the time available and are all very well up to a point, but you cannot remember everything after the event.

Some last a long while or there may be several in a series, so it makes sense to record them to provide a reference for future study. Not only that, as your collection gradually increases, the prints will always be there to provide valuable source material to which you may constantly refer. Themes often emerge when dealing with members of the same family. Patterns also occur in professions, in national identity or medical matters.

No matter how frequently you look at handprints, you will nearly always find something of interest missed in previous examinations. The old adage that one picture paints a thousand words rings very true here. Often, a series of events occur in an individual's life. If prints are taken at regular intervals, they will illustrate all the changes clearly.

Making handprints

To make good, readable prints of the hand you will need a small sheet of plate glass about 30 centimetres square (round will do just as well); a small photographer's roller (about 10 cms); plain A4-size white paper; a 5–6 cms diameter wooden rolling-pin, and a tube of black, water-based lino ink.

It is not advisable to try to use proper fingerprint ink as it is very difficult to remove afterwards. All water-based ink runs straight off the hands if held under a cold, running tap for a few moments; then the hands may be properly washed in warm soapy water. Cold water closes the pores so that ink cannot become ingrained in them: the hands can be cleaned quickly and efficiently. When you put your hands in warm or hot water, the pores are opened and the ink becomes ingrained and difficult to clean properly.

Making handprints can be a little fraught at first, but after a few practice runs you will soon make expert prints every time.

Squeeze out 2–3 centimetres of ink on to the glass plate and roll it out in an even consistency. Keep going until all the little bubbles and lumps have gone.

Use ink sparingly until you get used to it because the less on the roller the better. A thick consistency is likely to obscure some of the finer lines on the palm when you roll it out.

The hands to be inked should be clean because grease or cream can blur the result. Rings, watches or other jewellery ought to taken off, but remember that some people may be unwilling to remove wedding rings.

Roll in one direction at a time and gently ink one hand only. Try to include about 4–5 cms of the wrist area, and cover all the outer edges of the palm and fingers evenly.

Place a small tea towel or a hand towel on the table and put a sheet of paper on top of the the rolling-pin on the far side of the table. Place the wrist near the bottom edge of the paper and then roll the hand back over the rolling-pin. Ensure even pressure all the time and make certain that the thumb and fingertips also print out clearly.

Lift the paper cleanly away from the hand and you should have a perfect print. Always take the hand from the print, never the paper from the hand.

If necessary, thumb prints may be taken separately. Simply place the paper near the edge of the table and put the thumb tip on the bottom edge and roll in one direction only or it will smudge.

If, for some reason, the roller method cannot be used, place the folded tea towel under the paper and position the hand squarely on the paper and the towel. Then press gently in the middle of the palm and at the fingertips.

Now, carefully hold the paper at each of the four corners and ask your client to lift his or her hands swiftly upward. If this does not work, the "slap" method should be used. This time, place the paper on the towel and have the subject hold the hand about 15–20 centimetres above the paper. Now ask the subject to slap the paper quickly and firmly, straight down and straight up again, but remember to hold the paper still at each corner.

Lipstick or any other similar marking facility available at the time may be used, so experiment with a few "takes" first. However, you are liable to have problems cleaning up afterwards.

When all else fails, try a few practise runs on an ordinary flatbed photocopier. Cover the back of the hand with a towel or other cloth to block out light. Adjust the brightness facility to suit.

However you make a copy of a hand, *always* clearly mark it LEFT or RIGHT, for some copying systems will reverse the image. It is very easy to make a mistake at this stage, so please take extra care. The descriptions you use should be consistent. The following suggestions will help:

A   General description of the back of the hand.
B   Colour and skin texture.
C   Nail descriptions.
D   Flexibility of the hand and fingers.
E   Knots and knuckles.
F   Peculiarities, scars or other marks, if any.

If you have none of these facilities available at the time and want to make a close examination of the hands, lightly dust the palmar surfaces with talcum powder, then gently rub the hands together. All the lines and other features on the hand should be thrown into better relief and easily seen. This simple little trick makes the task much easier when all else has failed.

Further Reading

Over the years I have amassed a large collection of books on the hand from a variety of sources and countries. Ideally, I would like to list them all here as recommended further study, but that is not possible.

The books in this short list were all published in the last 50 years or so and you will gain by their study. Any omission from the list is not meant as a slur, for all new works have something to add to our ever-growing fund of knowledge.

Benham, William G. *The Laws of Scientific Handreading*. Putnam, 1958
"Cheiro". *You and Your Hand* (Revised by Louise Owen). Jarrolds, 1969
Compton, Vera. *Palmistry for Everyman*. Duckworth, 1952
Hutchinson, Beryl, B. *Your Life in Your Hands*. Neville Spearman, 1967
Jackson, Dennis, B. *The Modern Palmist*. The World's Work (1913) Ltd, 1953
Reid, Lori. *The Art of Hand Reading*. Dorling Kindersley, 1996
West, Peter. *Life Lines*. W. Foulsham & Co Ltd, 1998
West, Peter. *Complete Illustrated Guide to Palmistry*. Element Books Limited, 1998

Index

Air Hand, 46–49
Ambition, 21, 71, 96, 97, 102
Angle of time, 136
    of rhythm, 136
Apex of mount, 133
Apollo finger, 58–65
    mount, 72
Arch finger print, 125–127

Back of the hand, 50–53
    appearance, 51
    colour, 52
    texture, 51
    mouse mount, 70
Bracelets, 15, 109
Breaks, 79, 96
Business, 45, 96

Career, 99
Chained lines, 86, 113
Chirognomy, 13–74
Chiromancy, 75–117
Circle, 79, 91, 113

Colour of hands, 52
    nails, 55
    of lines, 79
Composite, 127–129
Conic, 14, 22–25
Courage loop, 136
Creative curve, 70
Cross, 79, 113
Cross bar, 79, 112

Danger, 113
Dental matters, 91
Dermatoglyphics, 123–138
Diplomacy, 34
Dots, 79, 114

Dress sense, 27

Earth hand, 46–49
Elementary hand, 15, 38–41
Emotion, 100, 137
Empty hand, 80, 104
Family ring, 111
    loyalty line, 111
Fate line, 77, 97–12
Fingerprint patterns, 124–132
Fingers, 58–65
Finger set, 59

Fire hand, 46–49
Firm palm, 23, 36
Frustration lines, 109
Full hand, 80, 103

Girdle of Venus, 105
Green fingers, 136
Grille, 114
Gypsies, 9, 10

Hair, 51
Hand prints, 139–141
    making, 139–141
    recording, 139–141
    uses, 139–141
Head line, 77, 81–86
Healing, 91
Health line, 106–107
    mount, 70
Hearing, 91
Heart line, 77, 87–91
Humour, 135
Hypochondria, 91

Illness, 90, 119
Index finger, 58–65

Intellect, 81–86
Island, 114

Jupiter finger, 58–65
    mount, 71

Knots at joints, 60
Knuckles, 61

Lazy streak, 22, 24
Left-handedness, 78
Life expectancy, 118
Line of life, 77, 93–96
    fate, 77, 97–102
    head, 77, 81–86
    heart, 77, 87–91
    intuition, 107
    Mercury, 77, 106
Little finger, 58–65
Long fingers, 20–21
Loop pattern, 129–131
Loyalty line, 111
Luna mount, 78

Medical Stigmata, 91
Medius, 58–65
Memory, 136
Mercury finger, 58–65
    mount, 72
Minor lines, 103–11
Mixed hands, 15, 52–45
Modern hand shapes, 46–49

Mount of Neptune, 74
    of Pluto, 74
Mounts, 16
Music, 135

Nails, 16, 50, 54–57, 119
    bitten, 50
    colour, 50 55
    horizontal ridges, 55, 119
    longitudinal ridges, 55, 56
    moons, 55
    specks, 55, 56,
    white spots, 55, 56

Palmar patterns, 133–138
Phalanges, 15

Philosophical hand, 15, 30–33
Psychic hand, 33–37

Rajah loop, 135
Rascettes, 15, 109
Restlessness, 109
Ring of Apollo, 110
    of Jupiter, 110
    of Mercury, 111
    of Saturn, 112
    of Solomon, 110

Saturn finger, 58–65
    mount, 71
Sensitivity pads, 64
Serious intent, 135
Short fingers, 20–21
Simian line, 107, 107–108
Sixth sense, 107
Skin patterns, 123–138
Smooth fingers, 21
Soft palm, 24
Spatulate hand, 14, 15, 26–29
Special marks and signs, 112–117
Square hand, 14, 18–21
Squares, 115
Stars, 116
Stress, 110
Sun line, 76, 104
Sydney line, 85, 108

Tassels, 79, 116
Tented arch, 124, 130–131
Thumb, 15, 16, 66–69
Time, 118–121
Travel, 96, 108, 109, 136
Triangle, 117

Versatility, 43
Via Lasciva, 105

Water hand, 46–49
White lines, 110
White spots, 54–57
Whorl, 131–132
Women's health, 109
Writer's fork, 85

Zone of Mars, 73